BLOOD, SWEAT AND *Scones*

BLOOD, SWEAT AND *Scones*

Two Decades at Crook Hall

KEITH JAMES BELL

Matador
9 Priory Business Park,
Wistow Road, Kibworth Beauchamp,
Leicestershire. LE8 0RX
Tel: (+44) 116 279 2299
Fax: (+44) 116 279 2277
Email: books@troubador.co.uk
Web: www.troubador.co.uk/matador

ISBN 978 1788035 286

British Library Cataloguing in Publication Data.
A catalogue record for this book is available from the British Library.

Printed and bound by CPI Group (UK) Ltd, Croydon, CR0 4YY
Typeset in 11pt Aldine401 BT by Troubador Publishing Ltd, Leicester, UK

Matador is an imprint of Troubador Publishing Ltd

This book is dedicated to my family for all their support, especially my mum and dad for their enormous help and, of course, to Maggie without whom none of it would have been possible. Maggie also spent many an hour proof reading my writing and reshaping my ramblings. Although, now I come to think of it, she has spent the whole of her married life doing the latter. I also owe a debt of gratitude to all those people – employees, suppliers and visitors who have made our dream a reality. Thank you.

Chapters

List of Photographs

Preface

When your family home is a house that has stood for over 800 years, on a site which has been inhabited for a considerably greater length of time, your own mortality often enters your thoughts. When we moved to Crook Hall, a local historian Margot Johnson, mentioned that she was undertaking research in order to write a book on the history of Crook Hall. Our former neighbour, Pauline Smith, told me she too was considering writing a history of the Hall. I have the greatest respect for these people, and as I grow older I feel that I am not academic enough to write such a history. Maybe I am also too emotionally involved with the fabric of the building and its surrounds to do justice to such a work.

However, many people have suggested that Maggie and I have a tale to tell. We certainly have. It is a tale of our part in the history of the Hall and Gardens. It's not a history of Crook Hall and it's certainly not my or Maggie's biography. It is an account of our part, albeit a very small part, in the history of the site. A few grains of sand in a fairly full hourglass. This book is an insight into our psyche, motivations and the pain and pleasure of looking after a part of our country's heritage. There have been many challenges along the way, and no doubt there will be challenges to come but our time at Crook Hall has been, and continues to be, full of joy and laughter despite the blood, sweat and tears.

The chronological order may be confusing as those twenty-one years have gone in a flash. With so many other things to juggle, keeping a daily diary of events was never seen as a priority. Consequently some things may have happened longer ago than I recall. I may have forgotten other events altogether, sometimes a day washing dishes, followed by a day weeding, two days decorating and then three days greeting and taking entrance charges at the gate meant that weeks can hurtle past in a blur.

I hope you enjoy reading this account and appreciate the help I have had from Maggie, our family, friends and all the team members both past and present who have contributed to this work both intentionally and unintentionally. I would also like to thank all those people who have helped in making our vision for Crook Hall a reality. We could not have done it on our own.

1

OUR LINKS WITH
THE NORTH EAST

1973. I wake up to the sun shining through the crack between my curtains. My first morning at university. Here I am at Bede College studying for my degree. I part the curtains and there below my window lies the City of Durham, overlooked by the majestic Cathedral. In turn the buildings at its feet are looking up at it as if in adulation. The size of the Cathedral is only checked by the river which snakes around its base keeping it contained within the peninsula. Alongside it is the castle occupied by students, the previous castle occupants having long since left. I hear the Cathedral clock strike once, quarter past the hour.

Time I made a move, I think.

★ ★ ★

2017. I open the Georgian shutters of Crook Hall to see the same ageless Norman building lording it over an ever changing townscape. In that moment I think of the first time I saw Durham Cathedral and all that has happened to me in those intervening years. I look down at the walled gardens which lie below the drawing room windows, I see the first drivers parking their cars in the car park before heading off to work in the city. Work. Yes that's all waiting for me downstairs. I make myself a coffee and sit in the window seat as a south-westerly gust brings the first spots of rain rattling against the window panes. The dark clouds begin to roll across the landscape veiling the tower of the Cathedral. I take a few sips of coffee, it tastes good. My mind wanders back to my childhood and my memories of my first visit to County Durham.

★ ★ ★

At that time I lived in a small village near Hereford, in the West Country. I was five and it was the school holidays. My parents had just bought a new Ford Prefect, registration PMG 178. It was super. One of the few motor cars in the street. That summer we were going up north to see our relatives. The destination was 5 Thames Street, Chopwell, County Durham. I had seen it so many times on the envelopes I had helped my mum post.

Durham seemed a long way away so our visits were always quite an adventure. When the day came I could guess what was happening and where we were going long before I was told: Dad was already in a panic, stressed by his attempts to pack, repack and pack yet again the endless luggage into what seemed the ever diminishing size of the boot. I was warned by Mum not to ask if he needed any help.

"It will be all unpacked and repacked at least twice if not three times before we set off," she sighed.

She was right. I watched my older brother as he ignored Mum's advice and offered to help Dad, only to be met with his holiday snarl. Dad fought with bags and suitcases which seemed to have minds of their own and going into a boot of a car was not part of their mind set. How he wrestled. The more he grimaced and grappled the less likely it was that the brown holdall would sit still in its assigned position. It appeared to have an innate attachment to a square metre of tarmac on the road and continually sought sanctuary back there. My dad was very determined. He finally pushed the boot closed on top of the brown holdall and its friends. I kept my fingers crossed that none of us would need that boot open until we arrived at our destination. There was pride in my dad's eyes as he marched back to the house to announce the car was packed and it was time to go.

His face changed as I told him I needed to go to the toilet, my brother added that he was now hungry and Mum said she had another bag to put in the boot. I hoped she was joking but she was not. Dad fumed. Our three pairs of eyes had been focused on Dad's antics with such concentration that we boys had failed to recognise our bodily needs whilst Mum had forgotten her extra bag. Dad did not look happy. Once I had gone to the toilet, my brother had some bread and Mum was sitting in the front with a bag on her knees the engine burst into life. We were off. I now realise why Dad would have been stressed; taking two young children on a journey of over ten hours in a car without a heater or radio, on pre-motorway roads, would not have been fun.

There was no sat nav. My mum was the map reader. Dad would have failed her had she sat a navigation exam. The verbal fireworks continued as we traversed the many towns which lay between us and the North East. There were occasional stops to allow my parents to exchange words and give my dad the opportunity to grab the map and explain cartographical nuances to mum, such as which way was north. Verbal commentary from the driver continued throughout. Dad insisted he knew the way without the help of a map. He usually did. Why on earth they had the map at all was beyond me. However, we two boys in the back were amused by our parents' antics which helped to keep us entertained throughout the trip.

After a gruelling journey with endless games of 'I Spy' and family map reading lessons, we arrived in the North East. We could always tell when we had arrived in Durham. Our nostrils filled with the smell of coal. Out of the window the view started to take on a grey hue as the smoke extracted the colour from everything it touched. Alongside the roads were large coal and spoil heaps and huge diggers acting as spoons stirring the coal and slag. The coal dust was hanging in the air, darkening everything it touched. The doors and windows of the houses had blackened edges. You even noticed the older men whose wrinkles seemed to stand out as if edged by coal dust. On many of our visits to the north we stayed with my wonderful Uncle Fred and Auntie Betty in Ashington. This was known as the biggest village in the country where everyone was dependent on the financial benefits of coal mining. All seemed to be happy to live with the environmental fallout from the pits. Every weekday morning you would hear the heavy boots of the men as they clomped off to work. The women left at home would often be hanging out washing that seemed to blacken in the breeze. Everyone appeared to keep themselves very busy.

What I really enjoyed in those visits to the North East were the warm friendly people we met whether it was in Chopwell or Ashington, this sense of belonging to a wider family. Everyone wanted to know your business and your business was of interest to everyone. There seemed to be no hierarchy. Everyone worked together and everyone was accepted as an equal. There seemed to be a genuine respect for each individual. A really strong sense of community which I have rarely experienced elsewhere.

★ ★ ★

My father had been born in Chopwell and joined the Royal Air Force in the 1940s. Whilst stationed in Egypt he met my mother. She was in the Women's Royal Air Force. They had a quiet military wedding and a year later my brother was born. They returned to England and, although it was a number of years after the war, there was still a housing shortage so the three of them lived in a caravan in Lincolnshire until I came along. Soon afterwards our family were on the move again, this time to the Midlands, then to Hereford and finally, when I was ten, to West Wales. Despite our itinerant existence we always retained links with my father's roots in North East England. I was eleven when my brother and I went to boarding school in Blackpool. The following year my father accepted a posting to Hong Kong. My brother and I grabbed the atlas to see where on earth it was. A long way away. We had been told we could go out twice a year to visit them. In effect I would visit my parents six times between the ages of twelve and fifteen. One of the benefits of this was that I was to spend my other four holidays each year with my Auntie Betty and Uncle Fred in Ashington.

* * *

By the age of eighteen I had lived in ten houses which had been spread around the country but I knew my home was in the North East. That's where my heart was. On my brother's twenty-first birthday, I visited him at Bede College in Durham where he was training to be a PE teacher. This was my first visit to Durham City. As with many first time visitors before and since I found the view of the Cathedral totally breath-taking. At that time, struggling along the crowded pavements from the railway station to the college through the narrow streets filled with cars and buses, the whole town seemed so welcoming. I decided then and there that I too would be coming to university in Durham. I just needed those elusive A levels.

By the time I returned to Durham to 'study', my future wife Maggie was studying for her A levels in Cumbria. I had come to the city and found it very small after living in London and Hong Kong. Maggie arrived at Neville's Cross College to study English a year later and saw Durham as rather large compared to her home in the small rural village of Sedbergh.

Maggie had been born in Darlington. Her early schooling had been in West Auckland. Maggie's maternal grandfather worked in a Darlington Chemical Factory while her other grandfather was a coal mine manager. Her father was a farmer. All her extended family lived in the North East.

We met in my last year at university. Within a year we were married and had moved to a house in Carrville, just outside Durham City. Maggie secured a teaching position and I joined an engineering company in Sunderland as a personnel officer. These were to be our chosen careers for the early years of married life. We moved to the nearby town of Washington for a few years but missed Durham and shortly afterwards moved back to life in the centre of the city.

2

MAKING CROOK HALL
OUR HOME

After a career in personnel management I set up a management consultancy business and Maggie was a teacher working in the Child Psychiatry department of Sunderland General Hospital. We lived in Western Hill in a lovely Victorian terraced house in the middle of Durham City with our two children who attended local schools. Initially, I was able to operate the business from home but, as the business expanded, we began looking for larger premises and fortunately Crook Hall came on to the market.

We had first seen the Hall some years earlier. I had been looking at an old ordnance survey map of the city and spotted 'Croke' Hall. This was strange because I had lived in the city for at least fifteen years and felt I knew Durham really well. Now, looking at the map, here was a place which I had not known existed. The Hall was just around the corner, about a mile and half away from where we were living. My curiosity was aroused. We thought we would pay a visit. The Hall was not open to the public and we cheekily drove up the private road (something we hate people doing now that we own the place). I peeked over the stone wall and before me was a timeless picture that blew me away. Someone was working in a beautiful walled garden in front of a building which I guessed was early Georgian. The perennial borders were in full colour. Flowers were jostling with each other to catch the rays of the afternoon sun. There were many different types of roses and some of the climbers were spilling over the garden wall. It was a quintessential English country garden. I already had walled garden envy and now, seeing Crook Hall, this emotion was in overdrive. I was captivated. It was unlike anywhere else in the city. I was drawn towards the whole scene that lay before me. A masterpiece, a mixture of a Millais and a Monet and, like a well-executed landscape canvas, it just dragged me willingly into the painting. I felt at peace.

★ ★ ★

Ten years later, in 1995, we bought it.

★ ★ ★

When we came back to the house as prospective purchasers we received specific instructions as to where to park. We had to use the parking spot which was at the bottom of the Georgian walled garden. The first thing I noticed was the fancy name plate on the left-hand brick pillar. I pushed the black wrought iron gate open and there in front of me lay a straight stone path leading up to a traditional Georgian front door. On the left of this white door the nine windows of the Georgian house stared down at me through the leaves of the pear trees. Above the main door was a rather plain casement window and to the right were smaller mullioned windows peeking out through the rambling vegetation. What struck me was that the garden ran into the house and the house in turn seemed to grow out of the garden. They were just made for each other. This was the scene I had viewed so many years ago and now that I was actually in it, it did not disappoint. The perennial borders dwarfed us as we walked up the path, the fragrances were almost overpowering.

A knock at the door brought Mary Hawgood, the owner, to the door. A severe looking women with a school-mistress look about her. However, once she smiled and greeted us, that all changed and she was totally charming. We were invited in and shown to the first-floor drawing room where we were offered tea. At that time I did not realise how many famous people had made a similar journey. Wordsworth, Ruskin and Oscar Wilde to name but a few.

On our way to the first floor we climbed a very wide staircase and I looked at the beautiful carved and unusual balustrades. Entering the drawing room, the first thing I noticed was the magnificent view. I had seen the Cathedral from most directions but never from this one. We looked straight across at medieval Durham with the Cathedral standing immediately behind the castle.

I looked around the room, taking in the painted wooden panels and alcoves. On the ceiling was a plaster decoration of a bird in flight holding a basket. Down at the other end of the room was what looked like a marble fireplace with a mirror over the mantle. The room was so elegant. Whenever you are house-hunting your eyes are everywhere, imagining yourselves, your possessions, and your life taking place in those surrounds. It is sometimes said that you know almost immediately whether you want a house or not. Often just walking over the threshold says 'yes' or 'no' to you, then you spend the rest of the visit supporting your initial conclusion. I had looked at some beautiful houses which were not quite right for us. I already knew that this one was perfect. Both Maggie and I had such a good feeling about the place.

As Mrs Hawgood took us proudly around her home we failed to get our bearings. The house seemed to be a sprawling, beautiful, jumble of rooms. She took us into the minstrel's gallery to view the Hall rather than entering at ground level. I gazed down at the stone walls, the arched windows and the old beams. I was awestruck.

Mrs Hawgood led us along the screens passage into the gardens. The screens passage divided the open hall from the service end of the manor house. I could see that our guide was passionate about plants but my mind was still in the house, mentally exploring the house room by room. One room which stuck in my mind was the smallest one, now my art studio, with its huge Jacobean fireplace filling the room's entire north wall. It seemed to sum up the quirky nature of the place. So full of character. I was smitten and metaphorically had

11

already moved in. As we gave our farewells to our lovely hostess we returned to our car at the bottom of the front path. There in front of us lay the panoramic view of the city. We drove off in silence, both deep in thought, but I could see that Maggie had fallen for the place just as much as I had.

★ ★ ★

Once we had decided to buy the house we returned to have another look at the property. We drove up the private lane. On the left side was a rundown barn with no roof timbers in place. I discovered some time later that, had I driven up that lane in the sixties, the site would have been very different. We would have been in a real farmyard, the farmhouse, the granary mill, stone barn and the large mill pond on the left. In front of us would have been a large wooden barn and on the right side a dairy block where the cows would have been milked. Between the wooden barn and the stone barn would have been a range of stone and brick buildings, one of which housed a spinning jenny. A traditional rural setting and one which was rapidly disappearing from our English landscape. On our visit in 1995, only the farm house, granary and the ruined north barn remained. On the Crook Hall site everything was as you see it today, although the coach house had a storeroom and stable block which housed a couple of donkeys. As the new owners we were determined that we were going to look after this beautiful part of the North East's heritage.

Our purchase had begun. There was lots to do; an

offer to be made and hopefully accepted, a mortgage to secure, permissions to gain in order to run my consultancy business from the premises and, most importantly, a house to sell and solicitors and estate agents to deal with. It would take us over a year before we took possession.

★ ★ ★

The early owners of Crook Hall had chosen the site very well. It stands on solid limestone rock above the flood plain overlooking the meandering River Wear. The site was situated on a spring, the well is in the cellar. Whilst standing fifty metres above the river, it faces south west in the lea of a hill which protects it from those harsh north winds. A warm and cosy site with plenty of water. The latter was to prove so true in our first few months of our occupancy.

One of the things which makes Crook Hall so remarkable is the way it has developed over the centuries, with each successive addition to the house being partly built on top of the previous one. The result is that on the site are three eras of English domestic architecture, all merging into one fascinating house. Over the previous years some of the fields around have been transformed into gardens. It is very unusual for a small medieval hall still to be standing. Most have disappeared and their stones used in other constructions. To find one within a city is very rare indeed.

★ ★ ★

Our surveyor's report of the building was horrifying. It was a long read. There were so many reasons for us not to buy the place. The surveyor wanted to cover his back with this report and so highlighted all of the many defects of the building. After initial dismay, we began to be more positive. There was no subsidence, no wet rot, nor dry rot. It was OK we told ourselves. We even justified the poor state of the roof which was struggling to keep out the elements (and we were told the house needed a damp proof course). After all, with parts of the Hall having had centuries of the best and worst weather which England can offer, there were bound to be a few issues.

We were advised to employ a structural engineer to have a good look at the roof. It would have to be a good look. The roof was enormous, as expansive as a terrace of houses. There were four elevations on the Georgian house, four elevations on the Jacobean house and two huge elevations on the Medieval Hall and all the other smaller roofs in between. I should not have bothered. He did have a look at the roof but only two thirds of it. I discovered in the first few weeks of ownership that he had not spotted some soft beams which came to my attention when I hit my head on them. His report never mentioned these beams. We had his fee refunded. He was lucky that we did not seek further compensation but we were attending to more pressing issues.

In the meantime I discovered that Georgian houses do not need damp proofing and the damp we had was almost totally due to a poor and unnecessary damp proof course put in some years earlier.

★ ★ ★

Twenty years on we live and work together in a house which many visitors describe as idyllic. What began as a lifestyle business is now much more than that. Every weekend the premises host one, two and sometimes three weddings. We receive fantastic feedback and it is a privilege to share our home with so many appreciative guests.

Today seems such a far cry from the first nightmare weeks of our occupancy. We had decided to leave the children with friends on the night we moved in. Ian, who was twelve and Amanda, who had just turned eleven were a bit uneasy about moving home, especially into a huge, supposedly haunted house. We gave ourselves twenty-four hours to unpack enough to make their new home seem less intimidating.

We arrived at the Hall unsuitably equipped with a white rabbit, a border collie, a Cherokee Jeep and a small push electric lawn mower. We also brought two plants from our old home for our new garden, a wild geranium and a vine. For indoors we had some old furniture from Maggie's family including a painting of her great-great grandfather. As an amateur artist I brought along an array of finished and half-finished canvases, oil paints and brushes. We also brought a pot plant, an Aspidistra – a must for one of those old dark rooms we were moving into.

We had no idea what was in store for us. I was focusing on my consultancy business whilst Maggie was surveying the enormity of the buildings we were taking possession of. I saw her glancing at the kitchen, a tired looking seventies breakfast bar surrounded by orange cabinets and old matching tiles. She looked overwhelmed. She turned to me and suggested, "OK, perhaps you could start by mowing the lawn."

I think it was to get me out of the house and give her some space. (As if she needed any more space.) Well, we had a lawn mower so I hurried out to make a start. I returned fairly quickly, the grass was still long as I explained; "The flex of the electric lawn mower will not reach the lawn."

"Get an extension lead," was the next instruction.

"That's not going to work. Have you seen how far the lawns are from the nearest plug point in the Hall?"

We both realised we were now dealing with a new household on a completely different scale to that which we were used to. The large Victorian house we had come from was dwarfed by the size of our new abode. The largest room in our previous house was not much bigger than the smallest one in our new home. The kitchen was the size of our previous kitchen and dining room combined. We looked at the staircase which, although beautiful, was twice as broad as any stairs we had ever owned. We wandered around in total awe. There was a sudden shout from one of the removal men,

"Have you got a map of this place? An A-Z would do. It's so big I am getting lost."

I ignored him as we were interrupted by a crash from above. It came from the men who were struggling to carry our piano upstairs to the Georgian drawing room.

I was hoping that would be its final resting place, as were the men. I rushed upstairs to be greeted by six exhausted faces. The men sat hunched over, catching their breath and muttering to each other. They were worn out but the piano was in place.

We finally sat down to relax after an exhausting day. It was about ten in the evening. As with all old houses we could hear disconcerting sounds as the house settled down for the night; central heating pipes clanked, water gurgled through pipes and floorboards creaked.

Suddenly we became aware of strange new sounds which we could not explain. They seemed to be coming from the medieval part of the house. Maggie was getting spooked. I reassured her, saying we were just getting used to our new surroundings and there was nothing to worry about. She was less certain and, as I listened, I too became less convinced. We both began to get more and more nervous. She started to say she felt the place was haunted and she began reminding me of the stories we had heard. Did I not remember that the previous owner had seen a ghost? We felt increasingly alarmed. We then started hearing other noises; dull bangs, scraping and sinister sounding mumbles. That did it. We were now very scared. We knew the house was supposed to be haunted and we feared that supernatural forces were at play.

After a quick slug of whisky for courage I went down the stairs towards the noises. It was a long, fearful journey. With each step, the sounds were getting louder and my heart was beating louder still. The noise was definitely coming from the direction of the Medieval Hall. I reached towards the door handle, nervously turned it and pushed the door open. The room was in darkness but as my eyes adjusted to the gloom I could see a man in dark clothes walking across the Hall, illuminated by the moonlight that filtered through the window. Behind him was another figure in the shadows. I was horrified. Not one ghost but two. I felt my stomach reach towards my throat as my blood drained in the opposite direction. And then – to my enormous relief – I recognised the two figures as the previous owners. The couple we had bought the house from had come through the large screens passage doors to retrieve the last of their furniture which was still stored in the Hall. They had mentioned they were coming back to collect it but we did not know it was going to be that night. I was delighted to recognise them and rushed off to put Maggie at ease.

The next morning we walked around the gardens. Our border collie, Ben, loved his new home. He was darting from bush to bush, investigating every hidden scent. The gardens were vast. We bought the property so I would have a larger office from which to run my management consultancy business. Our priority had been the building and we had only given the gardens a cursory glance. We were overwhelmed as we walked around them, both in terms of their natural beauty but also with the enormity of the tasks which would be required to keep on top of them.

We returned to the Hall, wandered around again, and discovered a huge leak in the roof above the minstrel's gallery and another on the gable end of the Georgian house. We sat silently in the Jacobean room. The reality of what we had done hit us. Maggie broke the silence.

"I think we will have to move again, I don't think I can stay here. It's just too big. We won't cope."

I looked at her in disbelief. We had spent three years looking for a quirky property from which to run my business. We had spent eighteen months gaining permissions to run the consultancy from these premises. We had secured an architect and builder to convert the coach house into a two floor office suite for the ten people I employed. A temporary office had been set up in the room we were now sitting in. Our employees would be arriving the next day to resume work in a new environment and Maggie was letting me know she wanted to move. Oh, and I nearly forgot, we had a new, absolutely huge, mortgage.

If I thought that was bad, it soon got a whole lot worse. The December we moved in was the coldest for years. The temperature dropped to minus fifteen overnight. We tried to pump out more heat by turning up the two central heating boilers. It was just too much for them. They both broke down. I nearly did too. Our insurance had not been transferred from our previous address, it was Christmas Eve and we were freezing. We could not get a plumber out to deal with the central heating until after Christmas. My mum and dad had come to share our first Christmas in the new house. We all huddled around the coal fire in our coats telling stories as we tried to keep the Christmas spirit going for the children. Not an easy task.

The fireplace was splendid. It looked like white marble but was actually carved wood with two naked figurines on each side and a wreath of leaves stretched over the wide opening. Amanda, our young daughter, looked at the fireplace askance and let her mum know she did not want her Christmas stocking hanging from either of those naked ladies' nipples. Obligingly, Maggie tried to hook the stockings from two of the carved leaves. To her horror the whole edifice crumbled under the weight and fell in chunks onto the hearth. Six people huddled around a roaring fire in a now broken fireplace. It must have looked like a scene from some Dickensian novel.

Then it got worse still. The heating was not working, the temperature was plummeting and there was a copper tank without lagging above our bedroom. The tank froze and burst, sending a waterfall down through two storeys of the house and into our temporary office. No sooner was I dealing with that than there was a yell to let me know that there was water gushing out of the coach house and into the courtyard. My feet were now soaking wet and freezing cold. I frantically paddled around looking for the stopcock. I managed to find it and turned the coach house water off. At the same time, Maggie waded through the water to rescue our pet rabbit, Flopsy. We had put him in the coach house because we thought it would be nice and dry. How wrong we had been.

The flood in the coach house receded but there was still the deluge pouring through the ceiling in the Jacobean room and I had no idea of how that water could be switched off. Eventually I managed to locate a second stopcock and the gushing water abated. Maggie and I surveyed the sodden room in dismay. There was nothing for it but to set to with buckets and mops.

Now we were facing our first Christmas in our new home without heating *or* water. Maggie was totally despondent. I tried to put a positive spin on things by pointing out that we had plenty of coal and the electricity was still on. Christmas dinner was a challenge! Possibly one of the lowest points of our time at the Hall.

★ ★ ★

After Christmas things did get better. I had never seen such happy faces as there were when the plumber turned up with new boilers and all the gear he needed to mend the pipes. The New Year rang in the changes. Two new boilers, slightly higher temperatures both inside and outside, repaired pipes and rising morale in the Bell family. Although I honestly believe it took until the end of January to get the building warm again.

The better weather in January gave us the chance to take a look around the site in greater detail. What a property. What seemed like acres of gardens to maintain, a building which appeared to be falling down around us and a ghost to boot. With these early difficulties we realised that we would both have to work hard to keep our spirits up and feel positive about the purchase we had made. Throughout the years we have owned the place we have sometimes pinched ourselves not believing we could possibly own such a beautiful home and on other days kicked ourselves for being so stupid as to buy it in the first place. We are pleased we pinch ourselves more often than we kick ourselves.

We were now ready for Len, our decorator, to work

his magic. While I did most of the designs, he was a dab hand at turning those designs into reality. We built the new kitchen around the newly delivered Aga. The cost of the new Aga went with the whole kitchen budget so Len made shelving out of odd pieces of wood and various cupboards out of old wardrobes. Maggie had greeted the arrival of the Aga like an old friend. She spent her time hugging it. I think she was reminding herself how cold she had been throughout December. I swear that Aga was loved more than I was. I was less enthusiastic. In my opinion it was a very expensive heater and scone maker. The kitchen is still standing today, twenty years and hundreds of thousands of scones later. It is a testament to Len's excellent craftsmanship. He also repaired the wooden fire surround that had come away in Maggie's hand when she was hanging the children's Christmas stockings while trying to avoid those nipples.

Len continued his sterling work, decorating the house from top to bottom. In the bedrooms he discovered that all the front windows had shutters which had been painted into their boxes, and we were determined to re-open them. They were in perfect condition.

In the tiny garret room, soon to become my art room, we found a very small access to an enormous attic which was completely empty and was ideal to use as a storage area. We made a new access and within weeks it was filling up with empty packing cases. You could see that it had once been a living space with blocked up windows and fireplaces, possibly servant's quarters from the previous century. Some years later we boarded out the space and put in some lighting. We could then clearly see how many things we had accumulated. A few years ago, when we could not squeeze anything else into the space, we decided to hold a rummage sale. It was a great success. People loved sifting through the paintings, furniture, books and bric-a-brac. There was so much to buy it looked like a village hall sale. This has now become a much anticipated annual event.

The previous owners left a lot of rubbish to be collected by the local refuse collectors. I was keen to recycle. I found two battered wing back chairs which had seen better days. We rescued them from the skip and reupholstered them. They now make a great addition to the house. They are currently outside the new attic area which we have restored and is explained later.

Outside in the gardens we marshalled a team, including my mum and dad, and started a general tidy up. There was plenty to do. We were immediately embroiled in work, repairing leaks, replacing broken gates, making steps safe, replacing doors, clearing the site of unwanted timbers and debris and renovating the coach house into a two storey office. The latter was the priority. We had ten employees housed in an unsatisfactory temporary office set up in the cold Jacobean part of the Hall. One of the secretaries of our consultancy business was scared stiff of the ghost and was often left on her own during the day. She was desperate to move into the new accommodation. Five long months later she was able to do just that, much to her delight. She never went into the Hall again.

The builders who were converting the coach house into our new offices were a great help in the rest of the Hall too. They replaced a couple of windows which were rotten, made two large wooden garden gates, two sets of steps and removed a huge pile of rotten roof timbers to gain access to the front of the coach house. It was here they laid the large gravel area which we were to use as a staff car park.

I discovered how heavy green oak was when I saw two large men struggling to carry what appeared to be a rather small beam. This was for an urgent repair required in the minstrels' gallery, where water had been pouring in, resulting in a sodden beam which was on its last legs.

The construction team remained on the premises for six months after we moved in. They were extremely good, very professional and, above all, patient. Our dog, Ben, a highly strung border collie, plagued them. Since moving to the Hall Ben seemed to have three key pastimes: When he was not chasing rabbits, his favourite activity, he was waiting for the next train to come down the main east coastline which runs along the field behind the gardens. Whenever a train came into sight he raced along the gardens barking at it. Each time the train sped off he believed he had chased it away and was truly 'Top Dog'. His third occupation was harassing the builders. He stole their lunches from their haversacks. He leapt on any new builders in that over loving way that only a dog can. He managed to charge over newly concreted floors to greet them. In the end they had to relay the one concrete floor three times because Ben was so adamant that he wanted to leave his paw prints for posterity as if he was some Los Angelino celebrity. The builders loved Ben; I had no idea why.

Maggie was still beside herself, not yet feeling

like she was 'home'. One evening on her return from work in Sunderland she was spooked by hearing voices echoing around the empty dining room. I told her not to be so daft and accompanied her into the room to investigate. I changed my tune when I too heard voices. Voices coming from the wall. We seemed to be listening to a conversation. More ghosts?

Fortunately a more worldly explanation soon became clear. Much to our surprise one of the builders poked his head out of the fireplace with a very cheerful greeting. What a relief. We were delighted we could put a body to the voice. The builders had been removing the gas fire and had discovered a huge inglenook fireplace behind the wall. They had climbed in and had been standing in there exclaiming over their discovery when Maggie came home.

The builders had a number of skips delivered for their refuse. My dad, not one to miss a trick, felt the surplus wood could not go to waste. He was of the 'waste not want not' generation. He took on Amanda as his young apprentice and together they built a tree house. Not a platform standing high up in a tree but a palatial two storey residence with a stepped ladder to the upper house. All covered in with seats and tables inside. It was a work of art and Amanda and her friend Vicky were absolutely thrilled.

Not only delighted to have helped to build the place but also delighted they could invite other friends around for tea just like the grownups. Not to be outdone, Ian and his friend Philip were also building a tree top home in the large cherry tree which stood in the Solar Wing

Garden. Maggie and I wondered if both our children were preparing to leave the family home. Their houses looked so inviting. Certainly on assessments at the time these new structures looked more waterproof and weather resistant than the main house. However, that waste wood was waste for a reason and it just could not cope with the ravages of the British weather. The tree houses managed to last for a decade. As they started to disintegrate we could not really apply for European funding for restoration so we removed them as they were becoming a hazard for our visitors.

My mum and dad were such a support to us, not just during that first cold Christmas but also for the next eighteen years of our ownership. Over those years there was no stopping my dad. Every time he visited he attacked the garden as if there was no tomorrow. Out at first light, short meal breaks to refuel and then back out to work until last light. He had such an attention to detail. My mum used to help in the kitchen, on the entrance gate, around the house and, on nice days, out in the garden. Years later Maggie gave my dad a small photo album filled with photographs of his garden accomplishments from the stone wall surrounding the Solar Wing garden to the path across the walled gardens. The album included the pergolas, the garden gates and steps as well as the small pond and bog garden that he had made. He absolutely loved the gardens and enjoyed immersing himself in the task in hand. On days when we were closed to the public the only interruptions were the calls from Mum who came along with endless cups of tea. He was a child again and the garden was his playground.

On the days when we were open he particularly liked the guests who suggested that they would not be able to manage what he was doing because of their advanced years. He would chuckle to himself as he knew that they were usually much younger than he was. I did try to draw the line when he was over eighty and was insistent on painting the windows of the Georgian house from a ladder. I was wasting my breath – my objections were ignored. The only thing that stopped him working was the failing light. He lived in London. I am sure he spent most of his time down there planning what to do next time he visited Crook Hall. He would often arrive with the car full of the tools and materials he would need for that next job. When his health started to fail he could not bring himself to visit. I think he would have found it too difficult to look out from the house thinking of all the jobs he still had to do. I can understand this because there is always another job to do or project to embark upon at the Hall.

★ ★ ★

We were all delighted to see the first spring arrive. The previous owner, Mrs Hawgood, sent a lovely card to Amanda describing all the spring flowers we could expect to see over the coming months. She proved to be right and we were quite excited by the appearance of thousands of snowdrops, which acted as an advance guard for the battalions of daffodils which followed. The great magnolia tree flowered in the March. We all felt like children at a party just waiting for the next present the garden was going to reveal to us. There were many unusual plants and if I did not recognise one I almost ran to the books to find out what it was called. They were like new friends and I needed to know their names.

The previous owners had a passion for peacocks. The next door neighbours did not share this love and had been plagued by a noisy procession of these birds underneath their bedroom window at unearthly times each morning. The peacocks had gone but their huge cage and shed remained right in the middle of the garden, beneath the branches of the splendid beech tree. I saw it as an edifice which needed to be removed. It was one of the first tasks we completed in the garden. We left the shed in its position as a tool shed for a few years but it was eventually moved to make way for a fountain.

★ ★ ★

We bought Crook Hall as a place from which I could run my management consultancy. However, once in the property, the reality that the grounds and the house were far bigger than our personal needs would ever be hit home. We invited along a lecturer from the local horticultural college to give us advice on how to look after the gardens. I remember standing with him in the walled gardens, gardens which had existed for over 800 years and he suggested we should rip everything out and put down a lawn. He added that this was the only way we could stay on top of it all. It was at that point that I stopped listening to the 'expert' who was suggesting we tore up hundreds of years of history with a well-oiled rotavator. We had other plans.

At this time I was putting a good twenty hours a week into the gardens, mostly in the capacity of an unpaid labourer. I recall one day looking at the small border that had taken me three hours to weed. I stood up and surveyed the rest of the walled garden and then thought of the other gardens beyond the black gate. The light bulb came on and I realised we needed professional help. Someone who could concentrate on the gardens. A person with focus was needed. For the first time we looked to recruit a gardener rather than just enrolling helping hands. We found David. He had an interesting background and we felt he would make a great contribution. He joined us from Elton John's estate in Berkshire. He came along full of enthusiasm and was an enormous help from the very start. Having said that I never did become that man of leisure, I was still doing twenty hours, I was just avoiding those small demotivating borders. I soon realised we could put hundreds of hours into the gardens and there would always be more we could do.

Some of the doorways in the house were low, even for someone of my modest height. After several painful bumps I learnt which ones to duck for. However, it did not prepare me for the accident in the garden. I was labouring away and banged my head hard on the guard robe doorway. I shrugged it off. I was getting used to the bumps. I continued work with what I thought was sweat trickling down my face. When I went back into the house for lunch Maggie was horrified.

"What have you been doing?" she exclaimed. "Look at yourself in the mirror."

I wandered across to the mirror and almost scared myself. There was blood pouring all down the side of my head. The sweat was actually blood. I looked as if I had been in a battle. Maggie administered some first aid. I bravely told her it was only a scratch which indeed it was but I do hate the sight of blood, especially my own. Now I was aware of it, the scratch was hurting a lot. I gratefully took all the sympathy I was given and retired to bed with an aspirin and an ice pack.

★ ★ ★

The vegetable garden was totally overgrown, with autumn raspberry bushes bearing the most enormous fruit I have ever seen. The bushes were interspersed with nettles, also the biggest I had ever seen. Some work was required. We, or rather the gardener with some help from me, cleared the area. We planted some potatoes to clear the ground but more importantly acquired a huge greenhouse with a heating system. We now had somewhere to plant our vine. I was looking forward to gallons of wine. (I have never lost my ability to dream.)

★ ★ ★

We hoped our second Christmas would be less eventful than the first but it was not to be. While it was by no means as cold, we were hit by heavy winds which battered the front of the building. Crook Hall is quite high above the river and is vulnerable to the prevailing south west winds. Nature seemed set on disturbing our Christmases. The winds rattled the front of the building bringing one of the pear trees down, along with a large section of roof. While the children unwrapped their presents I was in the attic unwrapping polythene sheeting to keep the weather out of the roof space. A few days later it snowed heavily. We stood in the Medieval Hall watching the flakes coming through the holes in the roof and settling on the stone floor. Two years into our ownership we hankered after a well-insulated and warm home but now reckoned on it taking a few years to achieve such luxury.

★ ★ ★

That spring we had extensive roof repairs to the Georgian house, it was all we could afford; stopping the rain and snow coming into the Medieval Hall would just have to wait.

As one of the builders who was converting the coach house remarked, "You will need deep pockets to live here."

We glumly agreed. The problem was that our pockets were nowhere near deep enough. We ignored our rapidly increasing debts and soldiered on.

★ ★ ★

That summer we had the privilege of seeing the garden coming to life around us. That's not to say it was all

Pimms, strawberries and balmy summer evenings. One night we were awoken by extremely strong winds. You could hear the noise of the trees being blown this way and that. There were also ominous clattering sounds. I was thinking slates. We had already lost a few slates the previous night. In the morning I went out to see the damage; a fifteen foot lilac down in the front garden along with a large bough of a pear tree. Behind the Hall more trees were down including a fifty foot silver birch tree completely uprooted but held up by its neighbour. With little idea of what to do I rang two friends who had experience of large gardens. They came around straightaway armed with chain saws. In no time Graham was standing on top of the newly built tree house. This was a test for Dad's building work. Graham looked like a cross between Rambo and the Terminator as he tore into the branches. Dave was below logging everything that came his way. I took my usual default position of general labourer. We worked all day until the job was complete. What great friends. We were absolutely done for but, with grins of satisfaction, we viewed the logs which would keep us warm next Christmas if the boilers were to fail again.

★ ★ ★

The gardens provided a natural habitat for many different animals. An army of rabbits were occupying the site but they were not alone. One morning we saw three deer standing forlornly in front of the Hall. They looked as if they were missing the previous owners and wondering if they could see them through the windows. In the walled garden I saw a stoat sit up and point its white crest to the sky then run to ground close to a large rose bush. Underfoot I could see a large toad crawling from one sheltered stone to another. In a particularly damp place I spied a lizard wallowing in the mud.

In addition to these animals a variety of birds had made our garden their home, including barn owls, woodpeckers, tree creepers, gold-crests and jays. One night I looked out of one of the windows onto the garden and saw a large fox searching around for a suitable source of food for the evening. It then took a massive leap up onto one of the walls and disappeared into the next garden. I closed the shutters and thought how amazing my new home was.

3

FROM FAMILY HOME
TO OPEN HOUSE

Many people did not understand our decision to welcome strangers into our home. All kinds of disasters were predicted. They advised us not to do it and indeed some suggested that our senses had finally deserted us. Others were even less polite, but the common theme was our alleged mental instability. We thought we had little to lose. We had a huge garden to look after, not to mention a badly leaking Medieval Hall which we could not afford to repair. Had we not received a few phone calls from people who wanted to view the old Hall then perhaps we would never have thought of opening to the public. However, we felt an obligation to let these enthusiasts see the place and any income would supplement our future running costs. We thought we would give it a whirl and see what happened.

Maggie was the one who focused on the detail and always wanted every 't' crossed and every 'i' dotted. I, on the other hand, tended to concentrate on generalities.

She never felt things were good enough; I always felt they were fine, even when they weren't. Maggie often said that if it had been left to her, Crook Hall would never have opened because it would never be perfect. Left to me we would have opened but then quickly closed because it would be so far from perfect. The synthesis of our personalities led to this adventure. We kept each other in check or rather Maggie kept me in check and I encouraged her to take calculated risks. It proved to be a good combination – even if it led to some heated discussions.

There were plenty of things to do before we could open the doors to the paying public.

First we had to establish a new entrance. Our private lane runs past two other houses. The Cassels, who had owned the Hall up to the 1970s, had sold off these buildings, along with the lane. They made arrangements so that the new owners of the lane would maintain it whilst the Cassels would have a right of way and could use the lane for any access they required. This had been confirmed by the local planners when we had gained permission to run my consultancy business from the coach house. However, I wanted to be considerate. We did not want to bring all our visitors up the lane past our neighbours' houses. We explored alternatives, some creative thinking was required.

I had a brainwave. I discovered that the meadow which joined our gardens to the main road was up for sale. Maggie's fortieth birthday was coming up so I decided to buy it. I was very pleased with myself. I reckoned I was killing two birds with one stone – we could make a private entrance into the gardens at the bottom of the meadow and the newly acquired land would make an unusual birthday present for my wife. Unfortunately Maggie did not share my enthusiasm for the gift.

"Just how old do you think I am? Are you thinking of putting me out to grass?" she muttered ungratefully as she surveyed the admittedly desolate looking field on the morning of her birthday.

Next to the meadow was a large car park owned by Northern Electric. After lengthy negotiations they agreed to sell it to us and they gave us permission to occupy it prior to the paperwork going through. On this basis we went ahead and created an entrance from the car park into the meadow and set a date for opening.

The pace of work in the gardens increased. We all did a lot of sweating that spring. Eventually, with only a week to go, our gardener, David, declared we were prepared for opening. We heaved a sigh of relief. All seemed plain sailing until three days before opening day disaster struck.

We had paid the money to Northern Electric for the car park but I received a message from them saying that they had withdrawn from the sale, were not going to sign the contract, were returning the money, and wanted us off the land. Our main entrance was now closed. We had advertised the opening and, with three days to go, we had no public access. My initial thought was to dig a path through the hedge at the bottom of the meadow to the road, but when I looked at the ten foot drop from field to pavement I realised that even if we worked night and day it was just not possible within the timescale. The other problem, which was equally pressing, was the car park itself. We had believed we had ownership for at least the past month and with the help of some university students had cleared and burnt swathes of hawthorn and weeds. The car park looked less bedraggled and we had been approached as to whether others could use it. We had already agreed and issued parking permits to seventy people who were going to drive their cars into a car park on the Monday morning. A car park we thought we owned. I sat and thought.

I rang Northern Electric again. They were adamant the property was no longer for sale. After much pleading they agreed to lease it to us. I think their guilt over the issue was reflected in the rent, a pound a month. Crisis averted. We were now set for our grand opening in April 1998. At least it felt grand to us even though we were only opening on Sunday afternoons and Friday and Saturday afternoons during the school holidays.

I remember the first day we opened, well. It poured down, I was absolutely drenched but had been coached very carefully by Maggie on how to greet the visitors if and when they arrived. There were fifty-three in total. We will always be grateful for the support of those brave souls. They seemed happy enough. From these very small beginnings our business grew. Over the following seasons we extended the opening hours from just Sunday afternoons to a visitor attraction that operates every day of the year.

A few weeks after we opened, our gardener, David, handed in his notice. We were then frantically advertising for a replacement. We struggled to get a new gardener. We had plenty of false starts. One of them did not stay long as she suffered from hay fever. Not as strange as you might think. The site is surrounded by birch woods, fields, and of course a wide range of flowers. Even with mild hay fever Crook Hall could get you sneezing your head off at certain times of the year. I had had hay fever as a child and it returned with a vengeance after I moved here. There is certainly plenty of pollen. In those early years the fields around us were used for growing hay with the harvesters out twice a year. It's a shame they are no longer farmed nor used for grazing.

Finally we were fortunate to gain the services of a new gardener, Ian, who was leaving a factory job to forge a career in gardening. We were pleased to welcome him. Ian was a dynamic person. He attacked the gardens with great vigour. As he was completing one project he was already planning his next one.

Many of the visitors who came had not previously known that the Hall existed let alone that we were open to the public.

I remember saying to Maggie, "If I had a quid for every person who said they did not know we were here…"

She pointed out that we were getting two quid from every visitor, even from those who knew we existed. I said no more, just took their money. Maggie made sure each visitor enjoyed their visit and told their friends. Our business grew by word of mouth.

Once we opened, I discovered that there was an old mining village in County Durham called Crookhall.

I had never been there but it seemed that every tenth party that arrived at Crook Hall had been to this village on a wild goose chase. By the time they arrived at our gates some of them were not happy, having spent an extra hour in their cars and a small percentage blamed me personally for their predicament. I used to hope they would cheer up after they had spent a few hours in the tranquillity of the Hall and Gardens. More often than not, they did.

Directions to Crook Hall are not straightforward despite it being in the middle of the city. Even with today's sat navs people can get lost. People sometimes end up miles away. The record goes to a guy who came from London to buy some chairs from us. I had given him directions including the full postal address and post code. He must have decided to just type in the post code with no idea of the geography of England. He was due to arrive at 11am. At 3pm he rang and the conversation went as follows.

Lost driver: "I am here but I cannot see you."
Me: "Can you see the river on your right?"
"What river?"
"The River Wear."
"There is no river."
"There is, it will be to your right."
"No. There is no river."
"You are at DH1 5SZ?"
"Yes CH1 5SZ."
"No D, D for donkey," I could not help myself.
"I am at CH1 5SZ," he told me again.

"You are in Chester," I informed him.

"Am I near?"

"It's probably as far as you have already come. In fact returning to London might be quicker."

"Oh shit, I will go home and try again next weekend."

He arrived a week later to pick up what had now become fairly expensive chairs.

Many of our visitors asked if we provided refreshments so we opened a small café. We were habitual coffee shop visitors and we knew what we liked. But being a bit of a grump, I also knew what I detested; weak coffee or tea, thick mugs or cups, watery hot chocolate. Whether we chose coffee, tea or chocolate there had to be generous amounts and it had to be piping hot. Ginger cake or home-made scones were a must. We had a few china tea sets of no great value. Tea always tastes better when drunk from real china cups and they were cheap to acquire in those days before the current vintage craze. We had set to work before we opened, asking a friend to make the scones and another friend to make the jams. We sourced all the other ingredients on the basis of what we felt would be served in a café we would like to visit. One thing we did know was that few tourist attractions we had ever been to had a good café. We were keen to be one of the exceptions and never wanted our visitors to feel obliged to use a mediocre café with high prices.

Another focus of our attention on our visits elsewhere was the service. We wanted to offer five-star service as well as value for money. We did not want service where people were trained to speak the same words over and over again in a formulaic manner. We felt this could be perceived as insincere. We therefore tried to recruit people who were naturally people-pleasers and enjoyed looking after others. In this way our team would be genuine, natural and above all friendly.

Our backgrounds were in education and training. The hospitality industry was new to us. However, we knew the principles of instruction and felt we knew what was required in terms of customer service. We also had teenage children so we assumed we had the necessary experience to manage the young staff who took temporary jobs with us when on holiday from school or university. We were wrong. The phrase 'herding cats' comes to mind. Our staff were keen, or rather the ones who stayed for more than one shift were. Some failed my first test at the interview. This was simple. Could they match my pace as we walked up the slope towards the house? I walked briskly and I knew that if they could not keep up with me or were short of breath at the top then they were not for us. It takes enormous energy and stamina to work in a café and you have to be fit. The next test was the door test. We have a very narrow doorway between the utility room and kitchen and I observed how easily and quickly individuals could carry a loaded tray between these two rooms. Our staff needed to be fast and efficient.

Then of course there was the work ethic itself. Once the youngster started, this was put to the test. Some found it hard to turn up on time. One very posh student, having been late three times over the first three days, described himself as 'a bit of a sloth' when it came to getting anywhere on time. He was charming but the charm did not wash with us. He did not last. Another student, a Cambridge undergraduate, took her books to her post at the entrance gate and greeted every visitor as if they were an irritating interruption to her studies. Again, her time with us was short lived.

One girl, a friend of the family, worked on the entrance gate on a particularly warm weekend. We had very few visitors so I walked down to see how she was getting on only to see she had stripped down to her bikini and was lying on the grass soaking up the sunshine. I was aghast. She felt she was making the most use of a very quiet day.

In the kitchen the assumptions we made led to some interesting conversations. I had assumed that all youngsters could make tea and coffee. How wrong I was. I saw an elderly couple pouring what looked like slightly discoloured water from a very large china tea pot. I immediately asked our very pleasant waitress back in the kitchen what she had done. Evidently she had picked the largest teapot because she liked it best, a teapot which was big enough for six people, and she had placed one tea bag in and filled it to the brim with boiling water. The next day I saw a couple sitting at a table with a cafetiere of coffee, again almost transparent. I asked them whether everything was ok. They said yes everything is lovely but the coffee could be a little bit stronger. I took the jug away thinking it would be our very pleasant waitress again. No it wasn't her but another member of the team. This girl had put one teaspoon of ground coffee in the pot as this is how she made instant coffee at home. I was explaining how to make a cafetiere of coffee when, over her shoulder, I saw the third member of the kitchen staff washing up. Well that was what he was meant to be doing but his approach was incredible. There was washing up foam everywhere. It covered his arms and was spilling over the bowl onto the floor. Oblivious to the mess he was holding each piece of crockery gently and lovingly with a cloth. At least I thought it was a cloth but I could not be sure as it looked like a handful of bubbles. Either way with such focussed attention on each item we would be here until midnight washing the dishes from just three tables. I nearly screamed. Later that day I saw one of the staff hoovering and she remarked that the vacuum cleaner was very quiet and was not picking up very well. I pointed out that it had not been plugged in. That was it. My blood pressure could take no more. We decided that we needed to train these youngsters properly and employ a more experienced person to lead the team. Moreover, we now knew we could assume no experience or even common sense when dealing with young staff. The only way was up.

* * *

My dad pessimistically said that when people had been to Crook Hall once there would be no reason for them to return as they had seen the place. We had other ideas. We wanted people to be desperate to return and bring their friends and family with them. We wanted them to return because they had so enjoyed their experience. We wanted them to see the Hall and Gardens at different times of the year. We wanted all our visitors to be our fans and to shout about us and of course our scones.

★ ★ ★

During this period I was still running my management consultancy business. I was bowled over one day on a course I was running. I was having lunch with the delegates and one of them started describing a fantastic place he had taken his family to over Easter. It was Crook Hall and he described it in just the way I had hoped it would be experienced. He talked of all of his family enjoying it for different reasons even though they were of varying ages: The children enjoyed exploring the site. The adults enjoyed the beauty of the place and its natural peaceful atmosphere. They all loved the scones. After his lengthy recommendation I let him know it was my home. I was absolutely delighted.

★ ★ ★

Our philosophy was to welcome and treat visitors as guests in our home. Maggie made it clear there were to be no 'do nots' at Crook Hall. It was our home, our garden. We were not going to have labels on plants, no waste bins, no 'keep off' signs and no negative signage such as 'no smoking', 'no photographs', 'no walking on the grass' or 'do not touch'. We had been to those places which were littered with such signs and we did not like them. Our chairs were to be sat upon, our books to be read, our garden to be enjoyed and our lawns to be walked upon.

4

PROMOTING THE BUSINESS

The initial excitement of opening the Hall was infectious. Everyone was so positive about our plans. We had great support from the local Tourist Information Centre which was to continue until their inexplicable closure many years later.

Maggie was in her element, promoting us to anyone who would listen. She invited journalists from near and far to visit and write about us. The *Durham Advertiser* and all the other local papers helped us and we gained great coverage in some of the national magazines including *Country Life*. She appeared on TV, starring in a Granada Production called *The Uninvited Guest*. This was a slot on prime time TV. She shared the thirty minutes with the owner of Chillingham Castle. The programme was all about living in a haunted house.

I managed a little less, thirty seconds on BBC *Gardener's World*. As time went on our marketing and promotion became a well-oiled machine with regular TV coverage of our exploits. I took part in local radio programmes including several gardening features and a local *Desert Island Disc* programme.

My first media interview was memorable. A journalist came from one of the local radio stations and said he wanted to tape the interview as we walked around the garden. He was recording every word and every 'uh' and 'uhm' as he quizzed me on horticulture. The poor chap was clearly disappointed with my responses. I could describe the colours of the flowers but after that my knowledge was woefully sparse. When he finished he discovered that the recorder had not worked and apologetically asked if we could do the interview again. I was delighted, indeed the thought that it might not work at all kept me going. I was no longer certain as to why I had agreed to take part in something which was frankly downright embarrassing.

While the journalist struggled to get his recorder working I took the opportunity to swot up on the names of the plants he had asked me about. The recorder was repaired and we were off again. Second time round was a bit better as I answered his questions. I actually knew most of the answers. Thank goodness for technology which breaks down.

A few weeks later a colleague who worked in my business said she had heard me on the radio. She told me she had a radio alarm and was woken at 6.30am by my voice. She said she woke in a panic wondering what the hell I was doing in her bedroom.

As a result of this foray into the world of radio I was invited to take part in a gardening programme with another radio station but I drew the line when they suggested I could have a weekly slot. That would have been a step too far. We also became a setting for the mainstream TV programme *Ten Years Younger*. This was a programme where a waitress from a local catering company was searching for eternal youth and was being helped to shave ten years off her appearance. Our role was to eat a meal, served by her, at the start of the programme and another one at the end. It was a role made for me. In my short film career I did not speak a word. My plate was constantly replenished. It was wonderful. I made the role my own.

I also managed to arrange an in depth interview with John McCarthy on Radio 4's *Saturday Live*.

We thoroughly enjoyed all this activity and were happy in the knowledge that it was helping to encourage people to come along and visit us and experience the magic of Crook Hall for themselves.

One of our more recent marketing coups was an invitation to go for a walk with Clare Balding. She presented a very popular Radio 4 programme called *Ramblings*. The idea was that we would take Clare on one of our favourite walks and our conversation would be recorded as we strolled along. We had decided to showcase Durham City by walking along the riverside. In anticipation of the day we wandered along our chosen trail. We were shocked at the amount of rubbish littering the river banks and feared that a dreadful picture would be painted of the World Heritage site. Maggie was straight on the telephone to the council asking for it to be cleared up and explaining why this was important to the city. They responded immediately and organised a clear up.

The day came. Clare was absolutely charming. She

and the producer got to work straightaway. No coffee and chat, we were straight into it.

Walking around the city being interviewed by a celebrity was a strange experience. Unfortunately we had picked a big horse racing day and the bookies were in full swing. Clare had spent many years as a horse racing commentator. Individuals, many of whom were more than a little inebriated, were sitting on benches along the riverside looking at and then destroying or discarding their failed betting slips. Many thought their luck had changed when they spied us. There were drunken shouts and bellows of "Clare", some insisting on having photographs taken with her. Clare was very patient but this led to much irritation from the rest of us, as we had to have retake after retake. Nearly every drunk wanted to speak to her. The producer jokingly suggested that we had discovered Clare's core fan base. It was an interesting, albeit quite shocking, insight into the life of a famous person. By the time we got back to Crook Hall Clare was like the pied piper with a bedraggled group of fans trailing along behind her. She finally stopped, offered them all a final photograph and then encouraged them to disperse. Despite the interruptions we enjoyed our rambling and I hope Clare did too. The broadcast led to many new visitors coming to Crook Hall and no doubt Durham. It was a great success.

★ ★ ★

Marketing was in full swing from the moment we opened the doors to the public. The more we promoted the Hall and Gardens the more we began to research and find out about the house. The Georgian part of the house is believed to have been built in the 1730s on the site of part of the Jacobean house. The design of the stairs is significant in that this type fell out of fashion by 1800 so it gives a fairly accurate date for the house, as does the fact that the Hoppers purchased the site in 1720. The Hoppers were either excellent recyclers, a practice which I wholeheartedly applaud, or short of cash. The original house is believed to have been a four-storey construction with dormer windows in the roof. In the early eighteenth century window tax was prevalent so the Hoppers were able to demonstrate to the city below their immense wealth – twelve windows. However if you look around the back there are very few windows. It seemed that all the money went into showing off.

A feature of Georgian architecture was symmetry. The Crook Hall builders compromised such symmetry. The front elevation would have been symmetrical but they had to use the doorway that remained from the Jacobean building, although it was converted to a classic Georgian doorway. In the drawing room this compromise continues because the builders chose to use the footprint of the previous building, thus saving on a new chimney and retaining some of the pre-existing walls. The wall between the dining room and kitchen is definitely earlier than 1700, being constructed of rubble and hewn stone. The front elevation is two bricks in depth while the back wall is just one brick thick. This use of the previous building is evidenced by a vaulted cellar which predates Georgian times; so again, we can assume the foundations were reused. The top step into the cellar clearly shows that a floor has been laid over a pre-existing one.

In the drawing room there were originally two matching fireplaces, one of which has now been relocated downstairs. At one stage both had been removed and kept in an outhouse because they were deemed offensive (those nipples again!). After The Great Fire of London building regulations were introduced. Fireplaces were no longer allowed to be made of wood so these particular ones were painted to look like marble.

The height of Georgian rooms was also specified by the new regulations; 10 ft on the first two floors, 9 ft on the third floor and 8 ft 6 inches on the fourth floor. This was followed to the letter at Crook Hall. The six-over-six panes in the windows were very fashionable but were only put where they would be seen. Likewise there were fashionable shutters in the drawing room and front bedrooms but nowhere else. All the floorboards were reused from the Jacobean house. Unusually, all the doors had six panels rather than four. They had been acquired from elsewhere and cut down to fit the openings. You can see this by looking at the bottom of the doors. In the centre of the room is a dove holding a fruit hopper which is a play on the family name of 'Hopper' rather than a coat of arms. Maggie thinks it was a poor craftsperson who did this as the bird looks more like a bad tempered bird of prey than a dove. The alcoves in the room were added later and used to show off collections, a great pastime of the Georgian gentry. We follow the practice of using the alcoves to display old tea sets and teapots some, of which have been passed down through our families. It was in this drawing room that James Raine would have met Wordsworth and Ruskin and the local diminutive Count Boruwlaski, who was only three foot three inches tall. It was said that the Count would be lifted up to sit on the mantelpiece at times so he could hold court with his friends and be seen more clearly.

Outside the drawing room the staircase is classic Georgian with a carved balustrade on each tread and it goes up four flights even though there is no reason to have it on the fourth floor. This was either to impress the visitor or for future plans which were never implemented.

Thus a lot of what you see at Crook Hall was all front and designed to impress. It seems the Hoppers were followers of fashion without a budget to match but they did well; the end result is beautiful.

★ ★ ★

Opening your house to the public is a great privilege. Most of the general public who visit us are wonderful. Many appreciate that they are entering someone's home and treat it as such. Some even bring presents to add to the historical papers the Hawgoods have left with us.

Probably the two most interesting gifts were a splendid sideboard and some ancient books. The Redpaths, who lived here in the 1970s, phoned out of the blue and said they were downsizing and did we want a piece of furniture which they no longer needed. This was a sideboard which was in the Hall when they moved here and that they had taken with them when they left. They felt it might want to come home. It now sits back in the Jacobean room and is much admired.

Another person got in touch to offer us some books which were initially owned by James Raine who lived here in the 1800s. The books are now back home and can be seen in the display cabinets.

The Fowler family who owned the house for over one hundred years presented us with a history of their family which included photographs taken in the walled gardens. Real treasures. People are very generous. We have been given so many china tea sets, tables, chairs, plants, mirrors, coin collections and paintings. But above all visitors have brought their enthusiasm, good spirits and kind hearts and have shown a real sense of appreciation to us for sharing our home with them.

Other visitors have been able to let us know where some items from Crook Hall have ended up. A visitor from Canada told us that her uncle had lived at the Hall and had taken a snooker table from here across the Atlantic. Evidently he used to play on it when it was all set up in the snooker room which is now the kitchen. She described it and it sounded a superb piece of furniture which would not be out of place at the Crucible. Another person had tracked down a large refectory table which had a brass plate on it stating that it had come from the Hall. This is now in Cadbury in the Midlands. It's no wonder then, that when we arrived there was no furniture. We did bring some pieces with us and also had some made. I will not tell you which ones are the reproductions. I had to smile to myself when I watched one visitor admire a piece of reproduction furniture and say to her friend, "They don't make things like this anymore." I knew it had been made within the last month.

We were advised by friends as well as our insurers to be careful opening our home to the public. Some had visions of the public behaving like Vikings rather than genteel visitors. This has not been the case although we have certainly taken security quite seriously, with alarms installed throughout, and we have had a few unpleasant incidents. One day our takings were stolen. It could only have been someone who worked for us. We thought we knew who the culprit was. The police urged us to prosecute, but as all our employees would have had to have their fingerprints taken we were not prepared to give the go ahead. We did not want the rest of our hard working team to be treated like criminals. We just made sure that the suspect knew that we were on to him. He didn't work for us again.

As for customers, we once had a family who stole from our shop, almost clearing the shelves. We realised later that one of the daughters had been on the lookout as other family members secreted items in their bags. Security was heightened after that incident.

We used to try to suss out people who we thought looked suspicious, and I have got to say that appearances can be deceptive; I remember spotting four guys sitting at a table and talking intently. They did not look like our typical demographic – more like they were four criminals planning a bank robbery.

I got into position so I could eavesdrop on their conversation only to hear one of them ask his friend, "I think the mistle thrush is indigenous, do you?" There followed a heated debate about British birds. I could not quite believe it. Since then I have stopped second guessing.

I am sure there will be some rogues out there but most of our visitors are wonderful. People had advised us against having the public in our house, warning of damage and theft. This cannot be further from the truth. We have found that the vast majority of people are considerate, respectful and honest. Yes, we have lost a few books; a treasured one about weddings, which I admit was a loss, and one on Scottish tartans which my Scottish mum gave to me. However, I think in the twenty years we have been open, apart from the raid on the shop by the aforementioned family, we have lost no more than that.

On the contrary, we have had several people send money through to us after they had forgotten to pay in the coffee shop. In one instance a couple picked some apples thinking it was our apple picking weekend during which we give away free apples. When they got home and looked at our leaflet they realised that they had got the wrong day. They immediately sent us a note apologising for their mistake and enclosing more than enough money to pay for the apples they had taken.

The money we were generating from opening was much needed. It was all being ploughed back into the Hall and Gardens. We had some large bills to pay in addition to the normal bills most households face. Constant repairs and patching to the roof were required from the first year we moved in and were cripplingly expensive. Owning a grade one listed building adds additional costs to any repairs and any work has to be very carefully handled. We used some of the income to replace doors, windows and shutters which were all looking very tired.

★ ★ ★

In 2001 we re-laid the whole courtyard. When we arrived it had been a sloping concrete space covered with ivy. We had made it safe when we restored the coach house by building some steps and giving it a general tidy up. Six years later, we felt it needed a facelift. The work we carried out then can be seen today and looks as if it has always been there. One of our volunteers, a chap called Peter, built the little fountain.

5

DEVELOPING THE GARDENS

We had our work cut out developing new areas such as the maze, ponds and the Cathedral Garden, while not forgetting about the existing areas which needed continuing tender loving care. With only one gardener, Ian, on the books at the time and the help of one labourer, Maggie and I, together with my parents, took to shovels spades and forks to do our bit.

My father was Trojan building paths, gazebos, walls and the smaller pond. The rest of us had to put up with his endless monologues explaining his painstaking progress as he reworked his physical activity with words rather than a spade.

Our gardener, Ian, was a huge, young and energetic individual who had a good eye for design and who worked incredibly hard. He used to work with headphones on digging, planting and pruning to the accompaniment of heavy rock music. He made many fabulous additions to the gardens. One of his first tasks was to make the whole site rabbit proof. When we first arrived we liked to see the rabbits running around. Our pet rabbit even joined them (by chance rather than design) and we loved watching him cavorting with his new friends. However, one morning I went into the vegetable patch to assess the progress of the newly planted lettuce only to find that they had been completely nibbled away. I stomped around in a fury like Mr McGregor. After that the rabbits were less welcome.

Initially we had acres of lawn. I estimated that it took over twelve hours to cut it all and that was with a tractor lawnmower. It didn't help that I was not the best driver of this little red beast. Very early on I managed to put my foot onto the accelerator rather than the brake. This should not have caused enormous difficulty, just a quick readjustment of feet on pedals. Not this time though. I was driving it into the shed where we kept it. The accelerator was sharper than I thought it would be resulting in the tractor racing into the shed then crashing right through the back wall. It was only the newly constructed rabbit fencing that stopped me and half the shed from shooting into the field. A second occasion I frightened Maggie by staggering into the kitchen bleeding profusely. It was this experience and the time it took to mow the lawn that drew me to the conclusion that creating a pond and a maze would be a good idea. They would halve the time taken to cut the grass and the other benefit was that we could sell that little red beast which I had grown to hate.

Ian planted the maze and sunk the large pond. The pond liner arrived on the back of a lorry. It was huge and very, very heavy. How were we going to get it in place?

The driver asked whether we had a forklift; I said no but that we had a gardener. The driver looked very unsure.

Ian and I pushed this liner, which was the size of a mini car, across to the large excavated hole which was to be the site of the pond. Two days and much sweat later the liner was in place. A garden hose was taken down to the pond and with great ceremony the water was turned on. We left it on overnight.

That night Maggie woke me in a panic. She was concerned that the pond might be overflowing and would flood the city. On reflection this was rather ironic as centuries earlier the Crook Hall estate provided the water supply to the city. A previous owner of the Hall had been brought to task for cutting off Durham's water supply and here my wife was worrying about too much water finding its way from Crook Hall to the city. I very much doubted that the pond would be anywhere near full. However, she was insistent so I got up at half past one in the morning and dragged myself out to the pond or should I say liner with a puddle in the bottom. I reported back.

It took two weeks to fill the pond and we remain forever grateful to Northumbria Water for their contribution.

Our children loved the pond. They thought we had created a swimming pool. That summer they spent most of the time down at the pond in their swimming costumes with their friends and lilos making the most of it.

Our dog found another game – chasing rabbits around the pond. On one occasion a desperate rabbit ran into the pond and managed to swim across it only to be met by a very excited collie at the other side. I saved the rabbit and thought it deserved a second chance. I took it over the fields and let it go. No doubt it was back in the gardens that evening.

Sometimes I still pinch myself and wonder how we have been so lucky to live here. On a warm summer evening sitting beneath the elm tree down near the pond and looking across the gardens to the fields is a sheer delight.

Having a pond in a garden is not just about the aesthetics but also the wildlife it attracts; the heron each morning, the birds coming to take a drink each evening, the moorhen who has set up home in the reeds and the duck who comes every year to show off her brood. At closer quarters you can see the newts and frogs as well as the many insects including dragon flies and may flies. Maggie has seen kingfishers a number of times. I always fail to spot them. In the early days we had a large number of golden rudd, which on sunny days bask in shoals just under the surface of the water and then retire deep enough to avoid the prying eyes and piercing beak of the heron. One of the severe winters saw their demise. We have restocked the pond and, if you look carefully in the summer months, you will see the fish gliding between the water lilies. The pond area is one of our favourite places in the garden. We often sit there with our neighbours, Chris and Elaine, and share a bottle of wine or two.

★ ★ ★

Ian was not just a gardener who did projects. He could also turn his hand to some of those mundane gardening tasks. One day I found him scraping out the weeds on a herringbone brick path. If you have ever tried doing that job you will know that it is mundane to the extreme.

"Ian, how on earth have you the patience to do that job?" I asked him.

He did not hesitate in responding,

"I have no patience and it is extremely boring. The only way I can manage to do it is to imagine that the judges from Chelsea Flower Show are coming tomorrow and I want this path to win a gold medal. So it just has to be perfect." I strolled away delighted that we had such a professional working with us.

Our labourer, Alan, was a character. I first met him in my time as a personnel manager and knew him to be extremely hardworking. His reliability was unquestionable and was demonstrated when heavy snow hit the North East bringing traffic to a standstill. I opened the shutters at 6.30am and there, in the wintry scene, was Alan who had turned up thirty minutes early to clear snow. His knowledge of gardening was limited, even after he had worked with us for five years, but his loyalty and hard graft were unquestionable.

He found some of our planting ideas very strange. On one occasion he grumbled to me, "There are ower many flowers here you canna see where to stand. Canna see the grass for the flowers."

Another day he asked me, "Keith, what is that flower? It is very bonny."

"A snowdrop."

"Can I take some yam for wor lass?"

"Of course you can," I replied, "Just take some."

"That's grand they'll look champion outside wor house."

He then asked, "Have you any other colours rather than white?"

He was so hard working. I gave him a reference file with pressed weeds in, five in total including nettle and Himalayan balsam. Armed with his file and a variety of tools he rid the whole garden of all these weeds. We no longer have any Himalayan balsam in the garden. What a thorough job.

Less thorough was the job I gave him of mowing the grass maze. He cut a straight line from the entrance to the middle. When questioned he said he had found it too difficult to find his way in and out using the previously cut path. I had to explain that that was the purpose of a maze. After Alan's intervention the maze was no longer remotely challenging. It was the easiest maze in the world. Something had to be done. Ian decided to plant it up with cotoneaster which, unlike yew, changes colour throughout the year. Although the maze was easy at first it would become more challenging with each year that passed. Ian's design was circular which made it unusual. Alan continued to find cutting the grass in it a challenge.

I remember his help one day when my consultancy were staging a team build event at the Hall. We had set them a gardening quiz which included identifying the eucalyptus tree and stating where it came from. One of the teams decided to cheat by asking the gardener. They chose our labourer instead of Ian. Big mistake.

His response was, "That tree? Oh, it came from out of the back of Keith's father's car." They did not ask him any more questions believing that he had been well briefed. Alan. What a star he was.

Both these individuals made a great contribution to the gardens during their stay with us. Recruiting good gardeners is always difficult, although I operated on the basis that I needed someone who knew more than me which more often than not left the field wide open.

In the walled gardens we worked hard to reshape borders and cut back what seemed to be a forest of forsythia. Under one of the bushes I discovered a water feature, or rather a pond, filled with decomposing dead rabbits. I peered at it in disgust and wondered why the poor animals had followed each other into the water. How many dead rabbits does it take for them to discover that rabbits can rarely swim? My mind then returned to the immediate task of emptying this pond of its contents. It looked and smelt horrible. I looked desperately around to find someone to delegate the job to. There was no one. As I emptied the pond I kept wondering if I would ever be able to forget such an awful job. The answer is quite obviously not, as I am relating it to you almost twenty years later. I think I was slightly traumatised.

One of the more enjoyable tasks in the walled garden was reinstating a long forgotten path which skirted the rose garden. We wondered when it was last walked upon and who by. Perhaps the Fowlers, who had the house in the early 1900s, were the last people who wandered along it or maybe people from an even earlier age.

We found so many interesting items in our random

digging including a wonderful array of clay pipes, bottles and coins. One day we found a primitive looking clay tube. We asked the local council archaeologist what it was. He was very excited and pronounced that you could tell by the scouring on one side that it was a medieval drainpipe. I was fascinated. The following day we found a large ancient storage jar in the shape of a bear. The medieval drainpipe was in fact the left leg of the bear. I joked that he must be wearing drainpipe trousers. I did not dare mention it to the local council officer and I am sure he would not have appreciated the comment about drainpipe trousers.

Another item I dug up was an old inkwell. I wondered who had left it in the garden and who had been the last one to use it. Perhaps it had belonged to Violet Hunt who knew all the Pre-Raphaelites and was engaged to Oscar Wilde. A strong possibility as she was often here with her grandparents who rented the house. Her grandfather was James Raine, a well-known local antiquarian. The house and gardens were such a trigger for my imagination. Truly inspiring places.

Behind the Leylandii and privet hedges, and just next to the Shakespeare Garden, was a huge compost heap which had been commandeered by the rabbits. I think it was their HQ. We knew we had to take it back. We brought in our ground forces; a friend called Jo, her boyfriend and a number of family members. We dug and dug and dug until our hands were covered with blisters, levelling the area and making it more like it is today. Our gardener Ian then created what we now know as the Cathedral Garden, our newest garden at the time, and one we were all proud of. We had all sweated and toiled and we were very pleased with the results.

I bought some Victorian edging stones from a local auction to border the lawn. Bricks were collected from around the garden and these were laid out to create arched beds to reflect the shape of the Cathedral windows. Ian had managed the planting, choosing dianthus to provide a stained glass colour for the 'windows'. He also came up with a great idea to cut arches into the Leylandii hedging. The views of the Cathedral from this direction were awe inspiring. This was of course before the sycamores grew to the height they are now and the Gala Theatre, which stands on the other side of the river to us, was just a twinkle in a deranged architect's eye.

As the plants matured the garden evolved and changed. The Cathedral Garden is a good example. The privet hedge had had its day and is now replaced with yew and we have added an arch with a black door and sanctuary knocker. Malcolm, our gardener after Ian left, built the stone wall on two sides and planted the beautiful roses. The rose bush in the centre was removed as was the small hawthorn tree. The old apple tree fell over and could not be saved. The Leylandii hedging became diseased and one of our volunteers, Rio, removed it. Unfortunately, Rio had also sliced off the top of our pretty little cedar sapling whilst mowing but having seen him remove those Leylandii I could forgive him a lot. What a hard job. How he worked.

Thus the Cathedral Garden has had a complete facelift since its creation. It does illustrate the work which is carried out continuously to keep the gardens in the shape required for the visiting public. We used to do all this work in those quiet months when we closed in the winter. Now we are open all year round we have no quiet times. There is always a project on the go. It is always busy.

* * *

Although until the age of eleven I had lived in the country, most of my adult life had been spent in a city. Crook Hall is located on the edge of a city, but surrounding the property are fields and woodland teeming with wildlife. My first reaction to these small creatures was to get rid of any animal or insect which I deemed to be a pest. In the gardens, squirrels, moles, rabbits and magpies all had to go. In the house there were mice that had to be eradicated. It was war and I needed the weapons; traps, air rifle, poison, nets and fencing. In fact anything that was legal had to be brought to bear on the enemy. I had to get rid of these unwelcome and unacceptable guests.

This mindset changed after a few thought provoking events. The first one occurred the day after I had shot a magpie. In the fields I noticed a group of magpies visiting the very place where one of their flock had met their end. I can only describe it as a wake; they were coming to show their respect to the deceased. I felt very guilty.

Another incident was seeing the little baby rabbits which one of the gardeners had caught in the Cathedral Garden and had collected in a watering can. They were peeping out of the top like a Beatrix Potter illustration. So sweet.

Early another morning I saw a hedgehog hustling its babies along over the grass to a log pile. It could have been a scene from a Disney movie.

These incidents occurred over a period of a few weeks and I started to understand that we are only sharing this wonderful environment with them all. They have lives to live which are just as important as ours. They are here because the habitat suits them, just as it suits us. The barn owl needs the wide open fields, the moles need the grubs under the grass and the magpies need the smaller birds, just as the other birds need the insects. It took me a few years to work through my naked aggression and become a true country dweller. Although I still cannot give them complete right to roam.

One day we saw a swarm of bees flying into the property and setting up home in a hole just inside the main door. The bees send out scouts who seek out their new home and these scouts made the mistake of picking a poor location – our main entrance. We had to get a beekeeper to move the colony.

Our rabbit fencing keeps the deer and rabbits out of the gardens. The moles tend to stay off the main lawns, I am not sure why; perhaps it is easier to tunnel elsewhere.

There are limits to my acceptance though. I can still be seen chasing rabbits out of the courtyard and removing frogs from the kitchen floor. I have even rescued a mole who was struggling to burrow through dolomite. He was getting weary so I put him back on the grass.

I am perfectly happy seeing large spiders scuttling across floorboards and carpets. I don't object to seeing mice and squirrels as long as they are outside the house and well away from our outside eating areas.

Birds often get into the Hall. The ones that cause the biggest disruption are the larger ones. The first one was a beautiful sparrow hawk. I made the mistake of calling in the experts. A man from the RSPCA arrived. Well the phrase, 'chocolate fireguard' comes to mind. He was scared of heights and was not so keen on birds. Not surprisingly he failed in his mission to rescue the sparrow hawk. Eventually we enlisted the help of our neighbour's gardener. He arrived armed with a large net and succeeded in catching the bird and letting it fly free across the gardens.

On another occasion our Australian gardener helped me to rid the Hall of a large crow. The Australian method was different. Roger, with a child's fishing net, stood on a table as I encouraged the bird towards him. He then lunged towards the bird with his net. He had a look of a deranged butterfly catcher from a bygone age. This was repeated sixteen times, I was counting. It then dawned on me that this was a battle of stamina. Roger's method was to tire the bird out before he tired himself out and fell off the table exhausted. He just about won. The bird came to rest and was resigned to being picked up and escorted off the premises. Roger looked worn out but had a victorious glint in his eye. I came to the conclusion that Australians are in for the long game.

I must admit I am not over keen on birds when they are in enclosed spaces. Whenever we have birds trapped in the house help from any quarter is welcome even if they happen to be celebrities. Martin Shaw, star of the television series *George Gently*, happened to be visiting one day when he and his wife happily joined in our local practice of the 'get the bird out of the house'. He thoroughly enjoyed the activity and beat the time set by our Australian. Another well-deserved English victory.

Even the children got involved in this game. When they were teenagers we were away visiting friends for the day when we received a call from our son advising us that there was a large pigeon flying around the house. He remained on the phone for at least twenty minutes, providing us with a running commentary of his direction of his little sister's efforts.

He shouted updates down the phone such as,

"She's going in,"

"It's looking good,"

"She has it cornered," and finally

"Success. Mission accomplished."

We pointed out to Ian that he had done nothing other than be on the phone to us. Amanda had done all the work. He begged to differ and responded by saying that he liked this management role and felt he was a natural.

★ ★ ★

Since moving to Crook Hall, water in the wrong place has been a recurring theme. Whether it has been percolating through the walls in damp corners or dripping through the holes in the roof it's been the bane of my life and a constant battle.

One of the first functions we hosted was held on a summer evening in July, a charity event for one of the local schools. The evening was hit by a deluge accompanied by thunder and lightning. We were all dressed for a warm, dry evening and were unprepared for the torrents of water which raced through the large wooden doors into the screens passage. The lady serving drinks was paddling around in two inches of water. Maggie had to lend her some wellies.

I found myself crouched over a drain with my hand down it trying to dig out years of debris in order to provide a workable soak away. I was drenched. Someone suggested I looked like Bruce Willis in the action movie *Die Hard*. I pointed out that the only similarities were a balding head, a white t-shirt and a good deal of stress, which was not an act on my part.

One of the outcomes of this downpour was that the gutters and drains were tested to the full and any repair issues were identified. More expense.

The next water crisis occurred on our son's wedding day, when the River Wear flooded the road at the bottom of our lane. The wedding was to be held at Crook Hall and we were all looking forward to it.

When the river burst its banks Maggie began to go into stress mode but I optimistically (or naively?) asserted that it would be fine. I felt I needed to investigate the depth of the water so I went to get my wellington boots from the cellar. As I opened the cellar door I saw my wellingtons floating in two feet of crystal clear water. Now I really understand the term 'well up'. It certainly had. I was astounded. There are not many people who have a house sitting on a well but when you really think about it that is why the house is located here. The well is situated at the bottom of the cellar steps and is completely filled with rubble, so we are only ever aware of it on the very rare occasions when it wells up.

In the end we had a wonderful day, the wedding went without a hitch. Well there was one hitch. I saw my sister in law, Jean, our first guest, hitching her lovely dress up above her knees as she paddled towards the bottom of the lane. Fortunately for our other guests who came later, access down the cobbled street of Sidegate meant that no one else was really affected by the swollen river. There are clear advantages to being sited on a hill. I think if we were ever truly affected by a flooding River Wear the market place would have to be underwater along with most of the city between these two points.

★ ★ ★

The well water is always crystal clear. I can handle that. What I find difficult to deal with is dirty water from drains and sewers, but then someone has to. The first time we had a blocked drain I was alarmed to see a manhole cover apparently being pushed up by some unseen force. At first I wondered if it was by Ninja Turtles. I would have been happier to see them than what I did see (and smell) when I raised the cover. There below me lay the bowel contents of either an elephant or a great many people and I began to retch. I could not even look around for help. I was on my own. The Hall and Gardens were closed after a few busy days, the two coach trips and other guests having left me with a deposit I was not expecting. The show had to go on. There were more visitors coming tomorrow who, no doubt, would need to use our toilets. I knew what I had to do. Our neighbour lent me some drain rods but no helping hand. I then discovered the drain was too long. It ran under the building, down the garden, and into the lane. These rods would hardly reach halfway. I made a frantic trip to one of the big DIY stores and came back with another set of rods. Still too short. Now the shops were closed. No more neighbours to call upon. The coach trip the next day was an early one and I set my alarm to get to the shops when they opened at 7am.

That night I barely slept. One dream of blocked drains was followed by another of being chased down drains by rats and yet another of wading through excrement. Real nightmares. I woke up the following morning and it's one of the few mornings I did not bounce out of bed. The prospect of my first task was certainly not motivating. Armed with a third set of rods I managed to clear the drains so that they were free flowing. I cleaned all the rods and the area around the manhole just as Maggie was delivering her welcome talk to the visitors. All was well. In an old house this kind of thing happens occasionally but the first time is a bit traumatic.

Apart from the odd incident such as the drains debacle we rather enjoyed those early days. We had great feedback from our increasing number of visitors. Our scones received wonderful accolades. People wanted to know how we could possibly make them so different to the others they had tasted. They believed ours were perfect. We were asked so many times that we started selling our secret scone recipe.

★ ★ ★

The support we received, particularly from the local press, was very welcome and extremely valuable. We liked opening our home to the public. Maggie said that it was the only way she could feel comfortable living in such a big house. We wanted to generate some cash to help maintain the gardens but we also wanted to share this extraordinary listed building with the wider community. We quickly realised that our visitors were experiencing the place in the same way as we had on our first visit.

We wanted it to be an adventure for the adults as well as the children. An experience rather than just a place to look at. A sanctuary from a busy life, a destination for peace and tranquillity. Whenever we proposed any change to the business, however big or small, we always asked ourselves if the atmosphere would be enhanced by the change. If not we would leave well alone.

We wanted to provide a five-star service by employing five-star people. I know that if we receive poor feedback, as we very occasionally do, our employees are as upset as we are and are desperate to put things right.

When people have favourably compared our gardens with Chatsworth, Great Dixter or Sissinghurst and or our afternoon teas with Claridges or the Ritz we have been delighted. Such feedback gives us all a warm glow.

I remember our son, who works in London, ringing me one morning. He was on the tube going to work. He had opened the *Independent* to see a photo of our house. It was an article describing the top ten places to visit just out of a town, and there we were in a list with Hampton Court. Ridiculous but fantastic.

A friend contacted us; he had been in Los Angeles Airport. He had picked up a magazine and had been amazed to see an article recommending travellers to visit Crook Hall in Durham, England. Unbelievable. We were finally on the map.

Our visitor reviews were terrific. So too was TripAdvisor – it now listed us on par with Alnwick Garden as the best park and garden in North East England.

I realised we were no longer just opening the doors to our home but had created a destination which people were willing to travel thousands of miles to visit. We both loved the idea. All the blood, sweat and scone making had paid off.

6

GOOD TIMES AND BAD TIMES

Out of the blue, three years after we opened, the electricity board rang me and once again issued us with notice to vacate the car park which they owned. They had previously pulled out of selling the car park to us but had continued to lease it to us. This latest notice to vacate the land happened almost immediately after we had improved our entrance to the gardens. The implication of their demands was that we would have to make another entrance from the street up into the gardens. The present one crossed their land. To add to this pressure the electricity board had only given us one month to make it and it was not an easy task. We met the deadline and built a new stone stepped entrance with two brick columns on either side. This matched the entrance we had to close. We had a second wrought iron gate made to match the old one. I had designed these gates to reflect those already in the garden.

We also decided to purchase a bigger shed to stand at the entrance. Its function was to provide shelter for the member of staff who welcomed guests into the gardens. I was not going to make the same mistake that I had made when I purchased the first shed and I misjudged the measurements. At that time I had wanted to spend as little money as possible. You know when people buy a new sofa and say it looks so much bigger than it had seemed in the showroom? Well, buying the shed was quite the opposite experience. When it turned up it was tiny. The price should have given me a clue. When it comes to sheds you get what you pay for. Little money equals a little shed.

It looked like the Tardis from outside but unlike the Tardis became even smaller once you were inside. We immediately christened it the sentry box. There was barely enough space to stand in it. We looked to furnish it with a barstool and we sought a very slim person to join the team.

Our plans to replace the sentry box were drawn up almost immediately. I also sharpened up my measurement skills. When the new shed arrived it was just as I had measured. It was spacious. A table and two chairs were easily accommodated inside and it had a porch. Luxury.

I was looking forward to welcoming the first visitors through our grand new entrance and volunteered myself for the first shift. A couple of elderly women came in. I let them know that we offered concessions. They both misheard and thought I had said confessions. They were a little taken aback but I think that with a little persuasion I could have had them sit down in this well-appointed shed and confess to goodness knows what.

Continuing the story of the electricity board which had served us with notice to vacate the land; this was a really big blow to us. The income which we had been receiving from the car park was keeping the Hall and Gardens going. Without it we had to ask ourselves some serious questions as to whether or not we could remain open. Although the business was increasingly successful in terms of popularity it was taking an enormous amount of our time and was still not financially viable. Once the salaries were paid there was very little money left. We did enjoy the process but we could not afford to lose money by remaining open without the supplementary income from the car park. After much discussion we decided to extend the opening times to weekdays throughout the summer in the hope that these extra days would go some way towards replacing the lost income from the car park.

In the meantime I made it my mission to buy the car park and, some years later, after lengthy negotiation, I finally did. Even though the purchase price was much greater than we had initially agreed I was delighted because it ensured that the land remained with Crook Hall.

The management of the car park provided us with some challenges. We had a spate of thefts culminating in someone having his car stolen. The car owner was very philosophical about it but I felt responsible and offered him a lift home. He then told me he lived in Northumberland, about a 100 mile round trip. That was a long evening.

The police, who were already involved because of the petty thefts, investigated the crime. They had a plan.

We would mount a surveillance operation. I was to park my car in one of the bays early one morning and keep an eye on the comings and goings. The police would then arrive at 9am sharp, park their car in my bay and continue the stake out.

It sounded really exciting.

We had already identified that all the thefts took place in the morning and the car park filled up very early so I took up my position at 7.30am.

I was still there at 9.15am. No police had arrived. At 9.20am a battered old car drove in. An ideal undercover car, it was a wreck. A man climbed out who looked just the part. Great disguise. I watched him wander around the car park. He appeared to be checking out the lie of the land. Good work. I guessed he was looking for me but had forgotten which bay I would be parked in.

I jumped out and ran over to greet the undercover police man. He looked at me in horror, dived back into the car and sped off out of the gates. It then dawned on me that he was the car thief. By the time the penny dropped another car, clean and gleaming, slowly pulled into the car park with two smart boys sitting in the front seats and gazing around. I went over and asked them who they were looking for. Turned out they were the police, twenty-five minutes late and missing their quarry.

Fortunately they had a plan B. This involved setting up a video camera at the window of one of our bedrooms. It would record all the activity in the car park. Surveillance 24/7. We were sworn to secrecy. Each day a person, not known to the staff, appeared at the Hall and Maggie showed them up to the bedroom so that they could change the tape on the video. The staff must have wondered what on earth was going on.

It was something of a relief when the thief was caught and the daily visits from the constabulary were no longer necessary.

★ ★ ★

During 2003 my consultancy business was changing. More of the team were working from their homes and we did not need as much office space. We decided to convert the two storey office into a ground floor office with a flat above which we could rent to holidaymakers. It seemed like a good idea but it was quite a task and a huge expense.

The holiday renting was an interesting activity. This was our first experience of renting out a flat. We'd anticipated people booking a one week holiday in Durham. It turned out that we rarely booked it out for more than a couple of days together.

Only one person stayed for a week. This man ordered a daily taxi to take him on a return journey to the bookies and spent the rest of the time standing in the car park smoking or inside watching the horse racing on the TV.

Most of the people who stayed wanted to be out of the house exploring our beautiful Cathedral city.

★ ★ ★

Maggie's life was even busier, as she juggled motherhood and several part time jobs; job one working in child psychiatry at the hospital, job two at the Hall, job three running a private counselling practice, job four lecturing in counselling at the university and now job five – cleaning the flat and washing the bedding.

I was busy running my consultancy which was increasingly taking me out of the North East, and then at weekends helping in the coffee shop and in between times managing the various Hall building projects and assisting in the gardens. Oh, and being a dad.

Our children needed more support. They were facing important examinations and education choices had to be made. We knew we had to find the time to give them the help they required. There was a danger that, with all our focus elsewhere, we might be disregarding the most important area of our life, our family. Our children had to be our priority.

We were both feeling overwhelmed by the whole Crook Hall enterprise. Something had to change.

We decided to rebrand the holiday flat as a permanent let which would ease the workload. Maggie resigned from the university and phased out her private counselling practice. We finally had some breathing space – but less money.

It was at this time that we decided that we could not wait any longer to replace the damaged Georgian roof, but I worked out we could only afford to reroof three out of the four elevations. The north facing one was in slightly better condition and by leaving this we could just afford to fund the rest of the work. When the scaffolding was up in the gardens and the slates were off I watched the slaters making light work of what looked like a very difficult job.

I wandered away to find somewhere quiet to have a cup of tea. I took a seat underneath the overhanging minstrel's gallery at the top of the walled garden. A good choice as it had started to drizzle. I sat with the tea and watched raindrops dripping from the large waxy leaves of the magnolia. I began to better understand and appreciate the work that the previous owners, the Hawgoods, had carried out. On moving here we had focused on what still needed to be done rather than what had already been achieved.

When the Hawgoods moved in, the Medieval Hall was half buried under rubble and soil. There was a huge hole in the north wall put through by the Fowlers so that they could use the Medieval Hall as a bottling plant. Not only had Dr and Mrs Hawgood sorted these things out they also added the beautiful turret which is such a wonderful addition to the Hall. They had managed to gain financial support for this project. Little did I know in that moment the great financial investment we would make in the years that lay ahead. Had I known, I may well have got up at that point, left, and handed the house keys in at the bank.

★ ★ ★

The children loved the place. The large rooms were built for entertaining and they took full advantage of the space. Ian, being the eldest, used it as base camp for his expeditions into Durham. More often than not on a Friday or Saturday night there would be many of his friends staying over. Maggie enforced some strict house rules, one being no shoes to be worn upstairs. So we used to count the pairs of abandoned shoes at the bottom of the stairs to determine how many of his friends were sleeping on his bedroom floor. The record was fifteen pairs. We slept at the other end of the Hall so we rarely heard them arrive back. They would heat up post-night out treats on the Aga and exchange endless tales around the kitchen table.

What I did notice was that some of the boys seemed to borrow each other's clothes. Their philosophy seemed to be 'what's mine is yours' or rather 'what's yours is mine'. Which is fine, but I did get annoyed when one of them entered the kitchen wearing my recent Christmas present – a Billabong t-shirt. He had helped himself from my wardrobe.

We would often find the boys' discarded clothing lying around. The attic was my art studio. One lunchtime my parents went up there to look at some of my paintings. They noticed what they thought was a pile of clothes left by one of Ian's friends with a mobile phone balanced on top. Just as they were remarking that the younger generation did not look after their possessions the pile stirred and out popped the head of Ian's friend, James. He peered at them with bleary eyes, let out a rather unearthly groan and then disappeared back into this pit. Alarmed, my parents left him to his hungover misery.

Amanda our daughter, who is a few years younger than Ian, seemed to live a separate life to her brother.

They are now best of friends but in their early teens they rarely spoke to each other. She had a small group of close friends. They used the upper part of the Jacobean room as a stage to put on Spice Girl shows which were very loud. Thank goodness karaoke machines were not around at that time. They sometimes spent all night trying to sleep in the supposedly haunted Jacobean room. I say trying to sleep because I don't think much sleeping occurred – more often than not they kept each other awake with ghost stories.

As she grew older her friends used to come round and spend seemingly endless hours getting ready to go out. Once she was away at university the visits home, although not as frequent as we would have liked, were always happy occasions. She would often invite her old school friends round as well as many new university friends. The house had plenty of space and it was great having it full of young people again.

On one occasion, when they were both home, one of Ian's friends from university took a shine to Amanda. He left Ian and the rest of the boys in a very cold Durham to come back to the house early. He had imagined staging a scene out of *Romeo and Juliet* but this fantasy was dashed by the first stone he threw up at Amanda's window. The stone crashed through the window pane and showered him with splinters of glass. His prepared announcements of love were greeted by silence. Amanda slept on. The unfortunate suitor was locked out of the house. Ian and his friends returned some hours later to discover the erstwhile Romeo hugging himself in the corner of a frosty courtyard, desperately trying to keep warm. A complete contrast to the scene he had envisaged but he was certainly pleased to see and feel the warmth of the greeting from his fellow students. Amanda was less pleased to wake up to find her windows shattered and a cold wind blowing through the gap. At least her dreams had not been shattered, unlike his.

Once our children left university they gained employment in London. No more long holidays home. The nest was empty. Not only were we missing them but also all their friends who used to fill the house up with their lively chatter. It became very quiet. Thank goodness for the increasing number of visitors.

★ ★ ★

When the children were younger we used to have au pairs stay with us and help with child care. It was lovely to have some of them return and visit us at Crook Hall. One of them ended up marrying a very famous French footballer. We had been invited to the wedding. Our famous footballer was a key player in the French national team who came to Durham in 1996. It was Euro 96 and the French team set up their base for the first rounds in Newcastle. Ian and I went to one of the matches.

One day I returned from work to find that our au pair had visited us and had brought her husband and his friends with her. Maggie had served tea to all of the French national football team. Maggie has no interest in football at all and the only footballer she has ever heard of was David Beckham. On the other hand I wanted to find out who was here. What did they say? What did they think of the place? Was Cantona here? Was Henri also here? I had loads and loads of questions but Maggie had no answers. Maggie, in a very appropriate French way, seemed to be very 'nonplus' about the whole encounter. I could not believe it had happened and I was astounded that it was so unimportant to her. I wished I had been there.

★ ★ ★

During the initial period of ownership we had the time to use the premises more socially than commercially. We loved using the formal Georgian dining room, especially at Christmas. When the children were younger we always used to invite Amanda's godparents and their young children round to celebrate Christmas Eve and exchange presents in front of the blazing log fire. This was always a lovely occasion.

On Christmas Day the dining table was reset for our family Christmas dinner. The furnishing seemed appropriate for a traditional family occasion. The room has a table and a Welsh dresser which has been passed down through Maggie's family as has the large press, a large cupboard with drawers below. The big oil painting, dated 1875, is a portrait of Maggie's great-great-grandfather. It was painted by John Horsborough, Fellow of the Royal Scottish Society of Arts 1835–1924, a Scottish portrait painter and photographer. He, along with his father, had painted people such as Sir Walter Scott, Robert Burns and Queen Victoria. Based in Edinburgh he was one of the leading painters of his day. We seem to know more about him than Maggie's ancestor. Maybe the furniture was originally owned by the great-great-grandfather. Since those early days most of the furniture remains the same but the function of the room has changed. It is now a tea room by day and a bar in the evenings.

The Medieval Hall was ideal for candlelit dinner parties and other functions. We celebrated my management consultancy's ten years in business, my fiftieth birthday and our silver wedding anniversary in the Hall. Amanda had a fantastic eighteenth birthday party and we had a great millennium bash. For those who remember, there was a lot of hype in the run up to the 2000 New Year's Eve. Not only because it was the millennium, but also because people thought there would be a worldwide computer crash, resulting in planes falling out of the sky, satellites failing to work, power stations becoming inoperable and communications grinding to a halt. For those who do not know what I am talking about, just ask your parents.

★ ★ ★

By 2007, we had over 300 season ticket holders and we had expanded our openings with many children's events and Christmas activities. We had also begun holding weddings and that Christmas our son, Ian, announced his engagement to Rebecca. A family wedding was planned for the following autumn. Increasingly, we found ourselves trying to juggle the management of a very busy visitor attraction with finding time for ourselves. We were beginning to feel the pressure again.

Crook Hall from the South

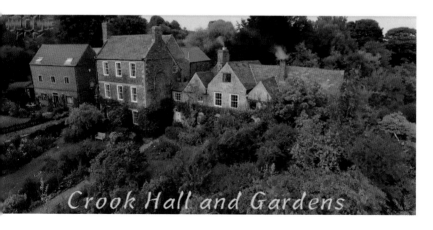

Aerial View of Crook Hall

Crook Hall from the North

Aerial View of the Maze

The View of Durham City from Crook Hall

Maggie and Keith in the Medieval Hall

Our son, Ian and his wife Rebecca, at their wedding

Our daughter, Amanda and her husband Mehdi,
at their wedding

Keith's parents, May and Harold, in the Walled Garden

The Entrance to the Orchard

Reroofing the Hall in 2009

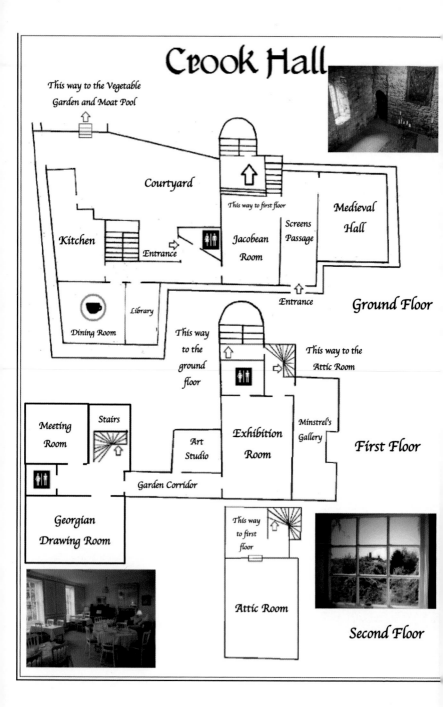

Crook Hall

This way to the Vegetable
Garden and Moat Pool

Courtyard

This way to first floor

Medieval
Hall

Screens
Passage

Kitchen

Jacobean
Room

Entrance

Library

Dining Room

Entrance

Ground Floor

This way
to the
ground
floor

This way to the
Attic Room

Meeting
Room

Stairs

Art
Studio

Exhibition
Room

Minstrel's
Gallery

First Floor

Garden Corridor

Georgian
Drawing Room

This way
to first
floor

Attic Room

Second Floor

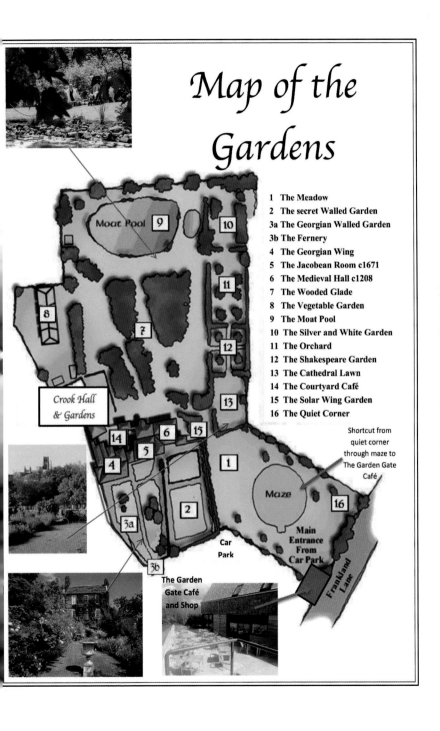

Map of the Gardens

1 The Meadow
2 The secret Walled Garden
3a The Georgian Walled Garden
3b The Fernery
4 The Georgian Wing
5 The Jacobean Room c1671
6 The Medieval Hall c1208
7 The Wooded Glade
8 The Vegetable Garden
9 The Moat Pool
10 The Silver and White Garden
11 The Orchard
12 The Shakespeare Garden
13 The Cathedral Lawn
14 The Courtyard Café
15 The Solar Wing Garden
16 The Quiet Corner

Moat Pool

Crook Hall & Gardens

Shortcut from quiet corner through maze to The Garden Gate Café

Maze

Main Entrance From Car Park

Frankland Lane

Car Park

The Garden Gate Café and Shop

The Garden Gate Café and Apartment

The Sleeping Giant

★ ★ ★

A few years earlier we had started providing food at some of our functions. We had no catering experience so we were on a steep learning curve. Maggie was a good cook, having hosted many successful dinner parties. I could make a mean macaroni cheese and boil a kettle but boiling an egg would be on the boundaries of my competence.

We found the functions very stressful and so we decided that we needed to outsource our catering. It was an interesting induction into the hospitality industry. One of our friends, a professional chef, helped out at a function but rued the day. This was to be his first, and last, foray into outside catering. While the event was a huge success, with all the guests thoroughly enjoying the evening, there was a lingering problem; the smell of fish. Although we had a team clearing and cleaning, one of the guests popped into the kitchen and offered the chef a 'helping' hand. Help is always welcome but on this occasion accepting it was a mistake. The guest was, in every respect, the friendly drunk. He praised every aspect of the evening with great gusto, and then offered to carry a few things out to the car, including a large urn of fish stock. He was unsteady on his feet. I watched him stagger, and I mean stagger, across the courtyard and through the gate. I followed him with some pots and pans. He managed to reach the open boot of the caterer's car and then seemed to have an inexplicable urge to empty the contents of the urn into the back of their car. I am sure it was an accident but it looked purposeful. He slurred out an embarrassed apology. The two caterers started to clean the car whilst encouraging their overly willing helper to leave them to it. Some months later I met up with the caterers who told me that they never did get rid of the fishy smell. The essence of rotting fish eventually forced them into an early sale of the car. I was left wondering who would buy the car. Perhaps someone who liked sushi.

★ ★ ★

Art has always been an interest of mine and moving to Crook Hall gave me a chance to have a space I could call an art room. Studio seemed rather too grand a term to describe the place. I set it up in the top room of the Georgian house. It had a real 'garret' feel about it. Amanda helped to decorate the walls with two huge murals; one of Van Gogh's bedroom at Arles and a more contemporary painting of my rugby playing brother. This dedicated space meant that I was spoilt, insofar as I could leave the oil paints out and half finish lots of paintings. Completing paintings had always been a difficulty. Now I could indulge myself. What's more, there was the potential to hang finished works around the whole building – there was so much wall space. Maybe I could even sell some.

What I did not anticipate was that each painting I wished to hang had to pass the hanging committee. This was composed of Ian, Amanda and Maggie. Few paintings made the cut but many found their way into the large storage attic never to be seen again. I did, much to my delight, make some sales and at one stage I was selling between twelve and fifteen paintings a year. When Maggie was marooned in America, which I will explain later, I painted fifteen copies of impressionist paintings in two weeks. I then held an exhibition of these fakes and ended up selling four 'Van Goghs' and two 'Monets'. I also sold three copies of Munch's 'The Scream'. Munch had painted four of these and one had recently sold for ninety-four million dollars so I was selling my four for ninety-four pounds each. I was left kicking myself when I sold one of them to a woman who then asked me whether I thought she should hang it in her Mayfair townhouse or her villa in Abu Dhabi. I just knew I should have added some noughts onto that ninety-four.

We wondered if we could extend my venture into running art exhibitions on a more professional scale. This would add interest to the house. We had organised some small scale exhibitions which had been well received but we felt we could be more ambitious.

We spent a few weekends visiting art galleries in the North East to try to find a gallery which fitted with Crook Hall. In Hexham we discovered a small professional gallery run by Ben Haslam. We loved his paintings. We asked Ben if he would be willing to host exhibitions at our venue. He did an excellent job for us over a three-year period during which time we sold a record number of paintings to our visitors, many being sent abroad.

Over previous years we had organised 'Art in The Garden Exhibitions'. These had been displays of sculptures which were placed around the property. The first one was featured in *Country Life* which was quite an affirmation. Art in the Garden brought in many visitors especially in August. In the first years we had some great sculptors. Among them was Graeme Hopper who gifted us the metal fish which we have standing in the fountain in the wooded glade. We were also delighted to welcome David Gross with his larger than life wooden carved masks which he later sold to Saatchi. David was a great support to us and used to come along for a number of summers and demonstrate his wood carving skills. Ray Lonsdale, who many may know because of his wonderful work in Seaham, was also a regular exhibitor.

★ ★ ★

Maggie would sometimes get in a panic about new events. She so wanted each one to be perfect. The fact I was seldom fazed, saying "Do not stress", "It will be all right" or "What's the fuss?" always led her to getting even more worried. It was almost as if she felt she needed to worry for both of us. On one occasion she felt there were not enough exhibits for the planned event. She then hit on the idea of living statues. She managed to persuade two of our team to volunteer.

Daniel, the first one Maggie spoke to, asked rather cautiously "Will I have to be naked?"

"No of course not," Maggie answered quickly before this idea took hold.

That would certainly have been beyond the call of duty. Daniel was advised that he would be in naval uniform and sprayed to look like a statue, he just had to remain very still. This turned out to be harder than we imagined. He startled a quite a few visitors when he accidently twitched as they were admiring him. We all became used to occasional screams echoing around the garden where he was stationed.

A girl also volunteered. Rest assured she was not naked either but her arms, legs and face were made up to look like stone. Our girl statue was quite indignant when a visitor touched her arm. At first she did not move but when the visitor turned to her friend remarking that the arm felt like really soft leather a faint snarl appeared in the corner of the girl's mouth. The visitors were terrified.

Our living statues did a great job and grabbed a piece on the local television news channel.

Some of our exhibitions were organised by a volunteer, Frances Thurlaway, and in 2007 she helped us win the Journal Culture Award for the Culture Event of the Year. We became a venue for the North East Potters Association as well as the Centre for Glass Sculptures. However, like many initiatives, they ran their course. We felt that the gardens were starting to take on a spectacle of their own and should be viewed clear of any distractions. That's not to say we have turned our back on having sculpture in the gardens, we still have a few pieces.

I must mention the piece which one sculptor left for us. It is a very large frog sitting on a stone and has been carved out of one huge piece of wood. It looks like something out of a fairy story. Maggie added a note inviting people to touch it and make a wish. Visitors are slowly wearing it away with each stroke. Our hope is that all the wishes come true.

Another cultural experience occurred on a glorious weekend of weather one summer. We were taken over by a film crew who were creating a pop video. We were really excited. The song sounded great and the two singers had appeared in the *Sunday Times* as 'the next big thing'. Such fantastic plaudits and the two would-be stars were very personable. The filming was a great success. However, the record and the video were never released. I can only assume that there must have been some falling out. I would have been interested to find out what had happened but our enquiries were met with a deathly silence.

* * *

One day I received an unexpected phone call from Ruth Ellis, the owner of Kepier House, the other grade one listed building in Durham City. She was upset as she had met some engineers in the field in front of her house who were surveying the land for a road that was planned. It was the first she had heard of this and wondered if I knew anything. I did not so she went on to tell me that the engineers had spoken of a plan to put a bridge over the river and a three lane road through the valley. I said I would investigate and get back to her. I found out that such plans did indeed exist and the road was to run around the back of Crook Hall, just behind the pond and then join the A690 next to the mainline railway bridge opposite Highgate. I was informed by the council at County Hall that all relevant people had been consulted including all 'hard to reach' groups. I pointed out that some of 'the easy to reach' people had not been consulted including the landowners and the residents of Sidegate, a street less than a mile from County Hall and adjacent to where they were going to build the road.

After this short, and somewhat terse, conversation I visited all my neighbours asking whether or not they had heard of this so called Northern Relief Road. They had not heard a word and were furious about the plans. Thus the campaign to 'Save our Valley' was born. We campaigned for almost a year with a lead group of campaigners made up of Peter Smith, Angela Teirney, Tim Clarke and myself, supported by an individual who did a great job of developing a website. We were helped by a group of local residents and the wider public, including many thousands of visitors to the Hall. Objections to the council plans came from far and wide. Letters were written to the local councillors, MPs and Euro MPs. We received funding for the campaign from a number of sources including Lush Cosmetics. The local press, including the Advertiser Group, were also a great support. We felt passionate about our cause. We had worked so hard at Crook Hall to create something special, a quiet peaceful oasis. Now there were plans to run a road through the fields which backed onto the tranquil gardens. It would change the atmosphere forever. We were frantic. We felt that if the plans went ahead we would have failed in our duty to protect the Hall during our ownership.

Eventually the plans for the road were shelved. I would like to think this change of heart was in part due to our campaign and the efforts of all those involved.

Other helpful factors were that the Olympics had sucked a lot of funds from public works and there were black clouds forming over the general economy. The danger had disappeared for the moment.

The threat to the setting of the Hall and Gardens was to raise its head again a few years later. The County Council Strategic Plan included pulling the surrounding land out of the green belt and allowing the building of what was described as low density housing. Local opposition was again marshalled to save the green belt from disappearing. This seemed to have been successful when the government inspector threw out the plan. However, the decision was subsequently reversed on appeal and the dangers to the site, whilst abated, have not entirely disappeared. We continue to argue that the importance of the setting of Crook Hall and its associated buildings – the farmhouse, granary and north barn – cannot be exaggerated.

★ ★ ★

When we first arrived at our new home all the fields around it were farmed by a tenant farmer. The scene took me back to my early childhood in Hereford. The farmer would have his large harvester cutting the grass. His helpers would all be there with the baler and I would be there with my wine watching all the activity. During other periods of the year there would be sheep, cows or horses grazing. He looked after the place very well, and when the tenancy was terminated the land was no longer farmed. It is now returning to scrubland.

We tried to buy the fields when the owner put them up for sale. Although we offered in excess of the asking price our offer was rejected and the land taken off the market. I was initially disappointed but very quickly this turned to relief when a huge hole appeared in the field. I went over to peer down into it. The hole was circular and must have been over five metres in breadth and about eight metres deep. It appeared to be an old mine working which had collapsed. It looked like a ventilation shaft. I reported the situation to the land owner and British Coal. Contractors came and filled the hole with concrete. Thank goodness there were no houses on the land otherwise there may well have been some fatalities or serious injuries. It was reassuring to know the Hall had been built on solid ground, a rocky sandstone outcrop.

At times we have felt the responsibility of owning a grade one listed building and the amount of work and investment needed to run a successful tourist attraction is just too much.

★ ★ ★

During a particularly bad month in 2007 we considered selling up and marching off into the sunset. We were exhausted, stressed and constantly worrying about the state of our bank balance. Perhaps it was time to cut our losses and call it a day. On the other hand we had already put so much of our lives into building the business, our visitor numbers were slowly increasing, it would be foolish to throw it all away.

We were at a cross roads. It was time to make some serious decisions.

I decided to book a surprise holiday to Paris. Our overdraft was already huge. A few more pounds would not make a difference. Maggie had always wanted to visit the city and it would give us an opportunity to think about the future without the daily demands of the Hall.

I expected Maggie to be delighted. She was not.

"Keith, I could not possibly go on a city break which involves lots of walking. I am exhausted."

"But I thought you would love a trip to Paris. You have always wanted to go."

"Not now. I just need a rest. Trailing round the streets of Paris is the last thing I need. The only holiday I want now is one that involves a lot of sitting."

"Ok I will book a different holiday."

I realised the romantic week in Paris was off.

Within a day I had booked a great alternative. A week in a luxury hotel, a converted monastery in Majorca. What a great holiday we had. Just what Maggie had ordered. The accommodation was amazing. A great blend of old and new. The new parts of the building enhanced the old and vice versa. In the bar a huge old olive press was surrounded by modern furnishings.

On the first day we sat and despondently thought of our English home and how different it was; leaking roof, broken windows, flaking paint. Plenty of the old but very little of the new.

We both accepted that we could not continue working ourselves into the ground. The particularly busy times, such as bank holidays, were manic. Our social lives were nonexistent. Friends were complaining that we never saw them. We had to review the sacrifices we were making. We had to make some changes. In the meantime we gave ourselves a pep talk – no more negatives.

We went back to Durham with renewed enthusiasm and determination. We would inject new life into the Hall. We needed to bring the house up to date without losing any of its charm or history. We did not know then but when all the work was completed we would return to the monastery in Majorca to celebrate our achievements. Until then there was a lot to get on with.

We started to implement the plan we had made in Majorca. We were going to extricate ourselves from all our outside work commitments and focus on making Crook Hall and Gardens a commercially successful business and not just a poorly paid side-line or hobby that filled up our life.

Apart from Halloween and Christmas, we were closed from the end of September to the week before Easter. This had suited us for a few years but staffing was becoming an issue. Moreover, the marketing we did one season seemed to have to be started all over again after we had been closed for six months. We decided to employ a few key people throughout the year. Their role would be to help in a variety of capacities such as managerial, marketing, administrating, catering, wedding planning and front of house. During the winter months when we were closed to the public, they would be painting, decorating, gardening and taking their well-earned holidays.

This meant that we were no longer totally reliant on a transient student population to staff our tea shop. We were going to build a business which would be able to outlast us. We did not want Crook Hall to become a corporate country house hotel but to continue as a family home which welcomes visitors. This is very possible, especially with a management team who can run it, with us very much in the background. The plan was hatched. Extricating ourselves from our other business had its problems but the job of finding the right people to run Crook Hall proved even more problematic.

We realised that the time had come to invest a considerable amount of money in the Hall and Gardens. We knew the building could be improved, especially for the weddings. One of the first things we tackled was the Medieval Hall; to make the roof watertight and provide a heat source. We decided to restore the attic rooms and chimney in the Medieval wing of the Hall and reroof the whole Medieval and Jacobean house. We had to make the whole building more welcoming. This investment decision was the reinvigoration we needed and we attacked the new approach with gusto. I scaled back my consultancy business whilst working with our chosen architect on the restoration plans and the work was to take place through 2009/2010. Maggie had already resigned from her part-time post at the university and closed her counselling practice. She continued with her work in child psychiatry which she loved. We felt it was important to have some regular income during these uncertain financial years.

As with all our projects, once we had decided on a course of action we were impatient to get started. I was reminded of the apocryphal story of the Chinese Emperor who, when describing an avenue of gnarled yew he wanted planted, was told by his gardener that it would take a thousand years to grow. The Emperor responded by saying, "Then we have not a minute to lose."

While I have no aspirations to be a Chinese Emperor, Maggie and I both shared his wish to just get on with things but we found that these kinds of initiatives cannot be rushed. First, we had to raise the money. More debt. Then it was essential to find a good architect. In the end we retained the services of the Cathedral architect. He was obviously talented but I worried that he might not be able to operate within our tight timescale. We were aiming for months if not weeks. My concerns were unfounded. He was a really sound project manager as well as a great architect. He helped us to plan the reroofing and insulation of the Hall as well as reinstating the chimney stack. We also realised that this work presented the opportunity to put in a new stairwell and restore the room up in the attic in the Jacobean part of the house. The alterations to the roof space helped to reveal the amount of recycling which was being carried out in seventeenth century England. The roof trusses and joists were salvaged wood from ships. You could see from the tenon joints and the shape of the beams that they had served nautical purposes in the past.

There was plenty to do. We had to take the roof off, put in insulation sheets and replace the roof slates with specially sourced new Welsh slates. There were custom made windows to historically match with the existing ones. The bricks for the chimney stack had to be purchased, which again had to be in keeping with the original Tudor additions. The gable ends had to be built up so the roof could be put back onto level walls. The quirky building was holding up the original roof at very strange angles.

During the work schedule the whole Hall looked like a large shed with huge beams being held up by props. There was dirt absolutely everywhere. I remember Maggie showing prospective brides and their grooms around this building site and painting a picture of what it would look like next year on their wedding day. Maggie's description was only matched by the couple's imagination of how their perfect day would pan out. They were not to be disappointed; the specialist Hexham based builders did a fantastic job and finished the work in time for our Easter opening.

One of the rooms we did not change was the avocado bathroom. This dates from the 1970s and is, in itself, part of the history of the building. We decided to decorate it with some of the posters I had designed while at university. One of the posters advertised a dance in the university featuring a band called 'The Scaffold'. Surprisingly one of the members of The Scaffold visited the Hall and he noticed the poster. We had a brief chat. I had another copy of the poster in the house which I gave to him as a memento of his visit.

★ ★ ★

Eventually, all the reroofing work was completed and the whole building seemed cosier. Despite this our heating bills were still climbing and always seemed enormous. I sought advice from others who ran larger houses. We were invited along to a presentation and seminar on alternative sources of energy. This was held at Castle Howard in North Yorkshire. I felt a little out of place as I was introduced to lords, ladies and knights of the realm. I became aware that not only did I have the shortest surname in the room but only one surname at that. I also had the smallest house. They talked of strategies to reduce their energy costs by hydro power, diverting rivers across their lands and laying acres of solar panels or harnassing ground source heat. I became more interested when they got down into the detail of draught exclusion and light fittings. I was less encouraged when they talked of setting their team of electricians on to this task and that task.

At lunch we were sitting in a beautiful dining room which overlooked the lake. I am not sure how the seating had been planned but on each table were five couples. Immediately opposite sat Lord and Lady Harbinger-Coutts. (Or that's the name I gave them.) He was dressed as if he had just come in from the grouse moors and had a vacant look as if he had mislaid his twelve bore. She was much younger, dressed more as if she was going onto a catwalk rather than attending a function about renewable energy. When Maggie mentioned that we opened our house to the public they both looked at us as if we had confessed to being carriers of bubonic plague. They were horrified. They repeated in unison.

'The public, oh dear how horrid."

They appeared to possess a deep seated fear that they might need to open their house sometime in the future. They saw renewable energy as a way of avoiding this distressing fate.

It was a really useful day. I came back home with a completely new mind set. We might have a problem but it was nowhere near as big as the ones I had heard about. It was manageable. I came up with a plan of installing solar panels on the roof slopes which are hidden in the valleys of the roof. This involved approaching various authorities to seek permissions due to the Hall's grade one listing.

I spoke to the local city council. They were really helpful and suggested that there were steps to cover first by making the house draught proof now that it was weather proof. We started to look at the detail. Our excellent contract plumber fixed a valve to cut our need to heat the entire house unless we wished to. The valve meant we could control the heat by effectively cutting the system in two. New radiators were put in and thermostatic controls fitted to all the other radiators. Our contract electricians replaced all the lights with more energy efficient ones. Our builder recommended someone who could replace our cracked and rotting windows. My dad had patched these up and painted them but the work was hiding the rot and there were holes and cracks in most of them. We had replaced two sash windows soon after we arrived but here were thirteen others needing replacement.

The man who was recommended to make the new windows was a disaster. On paper the scheduled work looked good; he was going to do one level at a time with minimum disruption to our visitors' experience and it was all going to be finished long before our Easter opening. During the first week of work we went away for a few days and when we returned we found he had deviated from the plan. He had taken all thirteen windows out at the same time. We were horrified. This impacted on every room. On three levels of the Georgian house there was dust everywhere and plastic sheets on every window. It was the middle of winter, freezing cold, and it catapulted us back to that feeling of misery we experienced that first cold Christmas.

As the project continued it was one issue after another and then, one day, the builder just failed to show up. He had walked off the job leaving all his tools. There were windows missing and his team had also disappeared. Always wanting to put a positive spin on things I was thankful the scaffolding was still in place. We were a few weeks from the scheduled completion date, and time was slipping away. Fortunately the builders who had initially recommended this 'expert' came along and, feeling very guilty, promised to complete the job with no charge. They did a splendid job and we did pay them. They deserved it and we were very grateful.

In those three years we had, with help from many others, seen off the road plans, reroofed the major part of the Hall and replaced all the windows in the Georgian house. The building and the site were in good shape. We were keen to safeguard the setting for the future and were determined that nothing detrimental would happen on our watch. With 800 years of history behind us we were only custodians for a very short period, but we needed to play our part and do the right thing.

7

OUR GHOSTS – THE UNINVITED GUESTS

We did not need the visitors to let us know we were living in a haunted building. There was enough written to get our goose bumps going, especially on St Thomas' Eve, the shortest day of the year, when our resident ghost is supposed to walk around our bedroom. We seldom slept well on that night.

Allegedly, Crook Hall is haunted by The White Lady. The front garden was planted with pear trees up against the wall by people who believed the trees would guard against evil spirits. The large wooden door has circular markings on, again to ward off evil spirits. Every effort seems to have been made to keep unearthly beings out of the house yet reports of sightings of spirits has continued over the centuries.

When there was a coal pit up beyond the gardens, mothers used to escort their children from the houses of Lovegreen Terrace to the pit head. The young boys, while brave enough to face the very real dangers of coal mining, were not prepared to pass haunted Crook Hall without their mums' reassuring presence.

One night the Hall had been set for a splendid banquet. The invited guests were gathered in another room enjoying drinks when there was a thunderous crash. The noise came from the Hall and the host went to investigate. On entering the Hall he saw all the tables had been turned over and all the table settings were strewn across the floor. No one had entered the Hall after it had been set. It was a complete mystery as to the cause.

The previous owner was certain she had woken up one night to find a woman in period dress standing at the bottom of her bed.

We have always had visitors who are keen to see or experience our ghosts. Many of our visitors have had experiences of feeling spooked and we have endless reports of orbs, often supported by digital photographic evidence.

One coach group rang up on their way home to tell me of an old man with a night cap who had been seen by many of their members on their visit. The phone call was prompted as they exchanged stories of their experiences on the coach. The caller, who I believed was just sending me up, asked if we had seen this strangely clad man, was he a ghost? I replied that we had no season ticket holders or visitors who answered that description so perhaps they had indeed seen a ghost. After he hung up the coach travellers either had a good laugh at my expense or were terrified.

On another occasion as I was locking up I asked a visitor if everyone had left the upstairs. She said that there were just two children playing up there. She added that they looked as if they were in fancy dress. I went upstairs and the whole floor was empty. No one could have come down without passing me. Another wind up?

We have had lots of strange incidents reported to us. One day a waitress was working in the Medieval Hall with her back to the far wall. She was totally unnerved when she felt a hand go up her shirt and touch her neck. She was completely on her own. She was so frightened that she ran from the room, breaking a glass and overturning a chair in the process.

Maggie had a similar experience when she was standing on the minstrel's gallery talking to a group who were gathered in the Hall below. She felt a tap on her shoulder and turned thinking it was a member of staff, only to find there was no one there. She thought nothing of it until later when one of the group said that she had seen a pale figure standing behind Maggie when she had turned away from the group. This person could identify the actual moment in the talk when Maggie had felt the tap on her shoulder. After this incident Maggie began giving her talks in the main part of the Hall, rather than on the minstrels' gallery.

When our dog, Ben, was just a puppy he had an extreme reaction to being on the minstrels' gallery. Maggie heard him whimpering up there so went to investigate. She found him backing into the corner with the hairs on his back standing upright. Maggie called to him and he started barking and bolted past her down the turret stairs into the Jacobean room where he stood trembling. Ben never ventured up to the minstrel's gallery again.

On another day a person Maggie knew through a mutual friend visited us. When she entered the Medieval Hall this women suddenly turned pale and began to shake and hold her side as if in pain. She walked over to the alcove and said she saw a soldier being killed by a man who lived at the Hall in a fight over a woman. She said the soldier's death had been hushed up and he was buried in the wall. She wanted to take the wall apart to find the body. Maggie refused to let her interfere with the fabric of a listed building but was taken aback by her sudden outburst.

A group of 'ghost busters' approached us to ask if they could mount a vigil by staying the night in the Jacobean room. We thought that this could lead to some useful publicity so we agreed.

They managed to terrify themselves. They were convinced they had seen The White Lady and that the portrait which hangs at the bottom of the haunted stairs was her. I told them it was actually of Amanda, my daughter, but this did not calm them.

They also reported that there were lots of smells which would suggest a ghostly presence – tobacco smoke for one but also a very strong smell of baking. The following day Maggie was able to resolve one of these mysteries when she took out a very burnt offering from the Aga. It was in fact the cake she had baked to serve to the 'ghost busters' with their tea and coffee but she had forgotten to take it of the oven. The smell must have percolated down to the Hall. We did not mention it. I have told no one until now.

One of the visitors told us that he used to visit the

Hall as a boy and he remembered the daughter of the family saying she regularly saw The White Lady on the stairs in the Jacobean room.

At the bottom of the stairs Maggie had invited youngsters to write letters to The White Lady. This was a great success and often provided an amusing read.

One young boy wrote, 'Don't haunt me White Lady, I am only six.'

Another one scribbled, 'You do not scare me White Lady. I am from Sunderland and no one scares no one from Sunderland.'

I had a few alarming experiences myself. The first event happened in December, on St Thomas' Eve. I awoke to a scratching and rustling sound on the other side of our alarmed bedroom door. It sounded like curtains being rustled, although there were none there. I had no supernatural thoughts in my head, quite the opposite; I assumed it was an intruder who would burst through the door any second. I reached for a suitable weapon and at the same time tried to wake Maggie from a deep sleep. I worked on the premise that if we were both awake and ready to run we could escape from this evil character. Then suddenly the rustling and scratching stopped and I could hear footsteps going slowly upstairs and then across the ceiling above my head. The sound was of feet walking across floorboards but I knew we had no floorboards in the attic above us, just plastic sheeting. Footsteps on plastic sheeting would not make that noise. The footsteps went right across the room and stopped just as I managed to finally wake Maggie. She had heard nothing so no collaboration there.

There was corroboration next time. We were preparing for Halloween and Maggie was holding the step ladders from which I was hanging some decorations. I made the comment that the candles she had planned to use may actually be dangerous and we should not have them lit this weekend with all the children visiting. She agreed she did not want any burnt children, but did not think the candles would be a danger. As I stepped down off the ladders they started shaking uncontrollably as if they had a mind of their own. I started to try to hold them still. Maggie accused me of trying to frighten her by moving the ladders. I took my hands away and the ladders continued to shake for a good minute. We were terrified. I tried to explain it away through physics but my grasp of the subject had been poor even when I had been spending three hours a week studying it. We ended up convincing ourselves that burnt children from the past had been sending a message to us. Perhaps we needed counselling.

The same evening one of our friends called in and we invited her to see the Halloween decorations. As we walked into the screens passage a bat flew past us at knee level. This had never happened before or since. We both felt as if Dracula himself was paying us a visit. Maybe we were turning into spiritual believers. My grandmother was a medium with the Northern Spiritualist Church. She would have loved the place. I wish she could have seen it, but then, who knows, she may have already visited us many times.

★ ★ ★

Although not a ghostly experience, we once had an uninvited guest who frightened us more than any of our spirit visitors. One night in September, about seven years ago, we were awakened just after midnight. There was a terrific noise coming from the front door in the Georgian house, a door we never used. It sounded like a battering ram being swung by a group of people attempting to gain entry to the building. No window overlooks this door so we could not see what was happening. I went downstairs naked and switched on the lights. (Neither action is to be recommended in such situations.)

Far from abating, the noise actually increased so I set the alarm off fearing that if these people were not scared away by my naked presence, lights coming on, or a burglar alarm, I was done for. The battering noise became even more intense.

I shouted "Go away." I can be very threatening.

I thought I could hear sobbing or crying. I checked to make sure it was not me. No. I am too tough to cry I reminded myself. I retreated back upstairs letting Maggie know these people were very determined. I told her they would probably be through the door within the next thirty seconds. The battering sound was deafening. Drastic action was required. I barricaded us into the bedroom by pulling the chest of drawers across the door and wedging two chairs behind it. I rang the next door neighbours and explained our predicament. We had hoped they might come to our rescue but, very wisely, they kept their doors firmly shut.

I called the police. Hearing my high pitched screams

begging them to come quickly, they assured me that they were on their way.

They arrived at the back door. We ran downstairs. The two policeman were brave guys. Armed only with a truncheon, one of them asked me to slowly open the door which was shaking from the battering it was still receiving.

For a person who has tried to watch *The Shining* four times and failed this was a difficult task. With one hand on the door handle and two feet firmly placed in the direction of my escape route, I slowly turned the handle expecting an axe murderer to take us all out. When the door was open there before us stood a very distressed, dishevelled girl. How such a waif of a girl had made so much noise was beyond me. The siege was over; I looked around to see if there were any cameras. Was this some kind of hoax? Maggie appeared from the library where she had been hiding. I found myself looking behind her to see if any famous celebrity was going to appear with a microphone. The story came out. The girl was a student, a fresher, who had got lost returning from town to her college. Whilst walking back to the college she found she was being followed by a man. In a panic she had scrambled over our garden wall tearing her clothing and losing her shoes and purse in the process. She had come up the path and was hammering on our front door. She was totally disorientated. The police were marvellous, both with her and me. Thankfully, I was not still naked and I was calming down rapidly. When all was quiet, and I returned upstairs, I discovered I could no longer move that chest of drawers which I had dragged across the floor so easily some hours earlier. Adrenalin. I slept well after that.

What I have learnt from all of this ghoulish business is that some people do see ghosts, at least they believe they do. Personally I am not convinced. I am always curious as to why they are grey or white ladies or monks, headless people or people in period costumes rather than punk rockers or shelf fillers from Sainsbury's. I have never heard of anywhere that is haunted by a hairdresser or a dentist. Perhaps I am just not well read on the subject or, more likely, a cynic.

Having said all that, when we had our bedroom in the Jacobean part of the house Maggie always moved elsewhere in the house when I was away on business. Maybe she knows something I don't.

8

TYING THE KNOT

Some of our friends had asked if we would host their family weddings. We always turned these requests down. We felt we were busy enough without adding wedding days to our events calendar. Moreover, it seemed a huge responsibility to plan and organise such an important day in a couple's life. We already had quite enough stress.

Everything changed after Simon Jenkins and his wife, actress Gayle Hunnicutt, visited the Hall. Simon was researching his new book *England's Thousand Best Houses* and wanted to include a section on Crook Hall. In conversation with Maggie he suggested that the Hall was an idyllic place to hold weddings. Its history and romantic setting overlooking a world heritage site would be a perfect choice for those looking for a unique venue for their day. He was very enthusiastic about the idea.

Although he persuaded us to reconsider our position we were still rather nervous. We knew we had much work to do. The first step was to liaise with the local council in order to gain the necessary permissions to hold civil ceremonies. The paperwork was daunting but our original perceptions of insurmountable difficulties were totally unfounded. We were fortunate to have fantastic support from the local registry office and the other council officers also proved to be very helpful.

What was more challenging was Maggie attending a course to acquire a licence to serve alcohol. She returned suitably qualified, but very concerned about all the custodial sentences she could serve for failing to comply with the numerous legal requirements. She was troubled by having to distinguish between those who were too drunk to be served and those who were just sober enough to order another drink. I felt this was an area I could provide help in. Spotting a drunk would not be too difficult a task as I had had four years of intensive drinking experience while at university. The only proviso was that I would have to remain sober. Finally, with all the drunks (I mean ducks) in a row we were ready to start.

We thoroughly enjoyed running the weddings. What a privilege to be present on these special days for such lovely couples. The wedding parties had the full run of the place, hiring the whole Hall and Gardens for the entire day. There was a certain self-selection and the type of people who wanted to be married in a Medieval Hall tended to be drawn towards the relaxed, informal weddings we offered. Arrangements were usually fairly simple. Some of the memories of those early weddings have stayed with me. No doubt the couples remember the incidents equally well, so no names in this chapter!

★ ★ ★

One of the most romantic moments was the time when a bride decided to arrive on a white horse. The idea was that she would ride side saddle up the lane to the Hall. She would be greeted by the guests and then slide off the horse into her future husband's arms. They say that you should never work with animals but this must have been the exception which proves the rule because it was absolutely perfect. She looked beautiful in her wedding dress which floated around her like something from a Disney movie.

Some weeks later I was talking to another future bride about her plans. I made the mistake of telling her about the bride who arrived on the horse. She thought it was a great idea and wanted to incorporate it into her day. Her fiancé pointed out that she could not ride. Now that entrance would have been a disaster.

★ ★ ★

Horses did cause a problem at one wedding. This was when three of our equine friends from an adjacent field jumped into the garden half an hour before an outside wedding was due to take place. They took up position among the chairs in front of the wedding gazebo, determinedly chomping on the grass. Fortunately for all concerned one of our team was an accomplished horse rider and was able to gain control of the horses and escort them off the premises.

★ ★ ★

Birds have caused us more difficulties. At one wedding the bride told me in confidence that she was having a hawk fly along the aisle to bring the ring to the best man. It was to be a surprise and she swore me to secrecy. On the day of the wedding the bride's mother popped in to see me and she said that she just wanted to mention the birds. I said I knew all about it and there was nothing to worry about. She said I could not possibly know; the doves she was going to release at the wedding were to be a complete surprise and she had not told a soul.

I thought this will be more than a surprise – it will be a bloodbath!

I imagined the hawk having its own wedding breakfast of tasty doves. I could not break a confidence but on second thoughts I just had to. I delicately introduced the subject of hawks and rings. The bride's mother was not to be discouraged and told me she would take complete responsibility.

I waited for the match of the day and was extremely grateful when the hawk did not turn up. A huge sigh of relief accompanied the best man's hand pulling the ring out of his pocket when requested. Not a bird in sight. The doves were released somewhat later and without any bloodshed.

On another occasion there was a wedding when an owl was used to deliver the ring. We were told that the owl had been well briefed. How you brief an owl is beyond me but come to think of it they are reputed to be very wise birds. This owl had been trained to go straight to the best man who would be easily identified as he would be wearing a black shirt. On the face of it this all seemed well thought through but no one had considered the finer detail.

Mark, one of the team, had a phobia with regard to birds and was wearing a very smart black shirt on the day. What an unfortunate coincidence. The owl swooped on Mark and perched on his shoulder. Not knowing exactly what to do Mark began to shuffle slowly towards the best man. He was terrified but to the guests it looked like a choreographed movement which had been planned beforehand and the ring giving went without a hitch.

Mark worked with us for about ten years and I do not think I ever saw him look more scared. His devotion to duty on every occasion was beyond doubt but this was a situation where his commitment was tested to the limits – and he excelled. Although from that day on he was always seen at weddings in a sparkling white shirt.

Another wedding couple had a hawk deliver the ring. The wedding was held indoors. Again not everyone knew of the plan. A lot of people are frightened of birds and the registrar that day was one of them. As the bird swooped down the aisle the registrar was the first person to spot the hawk. He moved extremely fast. He stood up and turned to retreat through the doorway immediately behind him. What he did not realise is the doorway was just that. No door, just an alcove. He hit the wall with a good deal of force and then turned back to the gathering. People often find other's misfortunes amusing and laughter erupted around the Hall. The proceedings resumed and the poor registrar was left with mortar on his face.

★ ★ ★

I remember another wedding where things did not quite go to plan. There had been a catalogue of mishaps before the couple even arrived. The groom's suit that he had had made did not fit him so there had to be some last minute alterations. The florist had got the wrong date so the flowers were not arranged in time. (We had plenty of flowers in the gardens so no problem in this area.) Finally, the ceremony was about to take place but the bridesmaids had not arrived. We waited. We waited. And we waited.

Eventually I was given their number and rang to find out where they were. It transpired that the two bridesmaids, who were both under twelve, were being brought along by their elderly grandparents who had got lost on their way to us. I got through to grandad who was driving. He quite rightly passed the phone over to his wife. In her panic she dropped it into her lap and forgot about it. I could hear her quite clearly, when the car stopped, asking pedestrians directions to Crook Hall. One after another told her they did not know. I was shouting down the phone,

"I know the way. Ask me."

I was ignored despite repeating myself many times in a louder and louder voice. Nobody, until the fifth pedestrian was asked, knew where we were. They finally arrived. Things were running very late. The registrars only had fifteen minutes before they had to leave for the next wedding. They could only complete the legal part of the proceedings so Maggie finished off the ceremony. She was in her element. All's well that ends well. It was such a lovely day and they were a wonderful couple. They will have some great tales to tell about their wedding day.

★ ★ ★

We did not have many weddings in that first year but the one we were really looking forward to was our son Ian's wedding to Rebecca. They had become engaged over New Year and had fixed a date for September. We were delighted with the news. Moreover, we also knew that we would be able to see a wedding through the customer's eyes so this was going to be an interesting experience. We were a little nervous. There was no need to be. The wedding was perfect. The Hall looked beautiful and our staff were excellent, we could not have hoped for better customer service.

Ian and Rebecca, who now have two children, visit us on a regular basis. We also welcome other married couples who return to celebrate an anniversary or just pop in to relive the memories of their day.

The one thing we could not guarantee on a wedding day was the weather and this always meant we had to have a plan B. Ian and Rebecca's wedding was the worst weather of that year but it was still a wonderful day. We now knew that poor weather was not a problem, we just need to be prepared for every eventuality.

★ ★ ★

However some things cannot be predicted and the weather at one wedding did cause some last minute drama. We had the worst floods in at least forty years. The river had burst its banks and the water was surging along the road below the Hall and creating an access problem.

Maggie burst into action. The wedding just had to go ahead. The rain stopped but it was more than a little wet underfoot. The water was too deep for our four wheel drive vehicle so it would not be safe for wedding guests to bring their cars through. We had to come up with another alternative. Maggie tried to persuade the fire brigade to ferry people through the flood waters in their fire engine. No joy.

After several increasingly frantic phone calls we managed to get a local farmer, Tom, to provide his grain truck to transport guests through the water to the dry land at the entrance to the Hall. We were rather nervous as a few weeks earlier he had delivered manure for the garden to us in the same truck. How clean would it be?

The guests arrived, parked in the large car park along the road, and were picked up by Tom driving his tractor which was pulling a hastily cleaned and decorated truck. It looked great. I helped everyone to climb up the ladder at the back. What an adventure. Footage of the escapade appeared on TV.

A couple with their young children arrived too late for the unconventional transport and I had to guide them through a number of hedges to get to the wedding. They ended up rather wet and bedraggled. At the end of the day their three year old was so disappointed that the water had receded and he had to go home the normal way that he cried. He made such a fuss that we indulged him by guiding him back through the hedgerows. Everyone had a great day and we will always be grateful to Tom for helping us out.

★ ★ ★

Quite often the men, whether fathers, grooms or brothers, seem to take a secondary role in this wedding arranging business. Sometimes they excel in these subsidiary roles. One father of the bride was instructed to look after a cask of beer which had been ordered. I am not sure whether or not he had experience in the NHS but he approached the task like a medic. He looked after this cask as if it contained some organs for a future, life-saving transplant. He arranged to come up one evening to put cold towels over the cask and tied on ice packs. The operation took a good few hours. He then returned and repeated the same procedure for two more evenings. When I was serving the beer at the wedding I was just waiting for people to comment on the drinks, not too warm I hoped. Everyone seemed happy with the temperature. All was well.

★ ★ ★

We used to let people bring their own food and wine to their weddings but we have had to put restrictions on this to ensure that quality is maintained. In one instance a couple had a number of bottles of wine left over because their guests had not drunk them. They kindly gave them to our staff. Unfortunately the wine tasted dreadful.

Next morning the staff all reported having had to throw the undrinkable wine out. All that is except for one team member who had drunk it, and who looked very much the worse for wear. After this episode we identified an excellent supplier of quality wines at reasonable prices who we now use all of the time.

★ ★ ★

Our food offering dilemmas took a little bit longer to resolve. We had some excellent outside caterers but others were less efficient. I remember when one wedding couple enlisted a friend to take charge of the catering. Eighty steaks cooked on a domestic barbecue. Slowly. It was close to winning a place in the *Guinness Book of Records* for the longest time between the first and last meal being served.

On another occasion a bride's caterer let her down by not turning up and disappearing with her money. We had to help to resolve the issue. It was all hands on deck in the kitchen that day. The following week we read a story in the press which named us in the headline and then described the incident. The headline suggested we had let the couple down, with no mention that we had in fact helped to save their day. After that incident we were more forthcoming in recommending reliable caterers and we have a secret blacklist of companies who we do not want to work here again.

★ ★ ★

We used to offer wedding ceremonies prior to 11am on Sundays. After this time the general public were allowed into the gardens. This suited couples who did not want to go to the expense of hiring the whole venue on an exclusive basis. They could just have the ceremony followed by a small drinks reception. A number of issues arose which made us come to the conclusion that this was not such a good idea: in one case a visitor arrived at 11am and paid her entry fee to visit the Hall and Gardens. She was very well dressed. What we did not know was that she had invited herself to the wedding. She sauntered in and joined the wedding party who had gathered in one of the gardens. She was very much the uninvited guest. She was known by the bride's family and had been excluded from the celebrations for reasons which were never disclosed. I had to let her know that she was very welcome to visit the Hall and Gardens but we could not allow her to mingle with the wedding party. It was a very uncomfortable situation for all concerned.

★ ★ ★

On another occasion I remember being woken by a phone call from a man at four in the morning. He asked me whether his wife was still at the Hall as she had been attending that day's wedding. Maggie began to get stressed. The Hall was all locked up, the guests had gone hours earlier and Maggie was worried that the woman could be locked in a room or even worse, collapsed in the gardens or fallen into the pond.

However, I recognised his description of his wife and knew she was no longer on the premises. I had seen her leaving with a high spirited group of men. I don't think that was what the caller was expecting. Another uncomfortable conversation ensued as I explained this to the increasingly irate husband.

★ ★ ★

Another awkward situation arose when I was making sure everyone had left the building after a wedding and came across a rather inebriated bride in the attic room. She was on her own. She swayed towards me and asked me to help her out of her wedding dress. I had improved my customer service over the years but I did feel this was probably a step too far. I said I would find someone to help her as I fled the room to search out her new husband.

★ ★ ★

Each wedding is bespoke. The themes and colour schemes are always different and the mixture of families and personalities all mean that each day is unique. For instance, we hosted a small Japanese wedding with twelve guests. The bride wore a traditional Japanese kimono. In order to attend, her parents, who spoke no English, had made a journey halfway around the world, flying into Newcastle airport on the Friday and going back to Japan on the Monday. By the end of the weekend we had not learnt any Japanese but we had all perfected a suitably polite Japanese bow.

* * *

One of the features of each wedding was the sheer imagination of the couple in planning their day. The fact that they take over the whole venue for their wedding means that their creativity can run at full throttle. The themes can be very imaginative; *Alice in Wonderland*, gothic, winter wonderland and even a festival themed one. On the latter occasion the groom had his name changed by deed poll so that he and his wife could be introduced as Mr and Mrs Fantastic. How crazy was that?

* * *

The work that has gone into some of the arrangements has been phenomenal. One couple had place settings made out of Lego characters which reflected the characteristics of each of their guests, such as a figure holding a baby for a new mum and a figure with a camera for a keen photographer. It was lovely when the couple also provided our two wedding coordinators with Lego figures of themselves as mementos.

* * *

Some of the place and table settings have been inspired by the couple's favourite place, their favourite movie or a favourite TV programme. The music choices were always interesting. A particularly memorable selection at one wedding was the film score from

Jaws instead of 'Here Comes the Bride'. You get a real insight into the couple on such a personal occasion. We are all different.

★ ★ ★

Even the names on the seating plans are interesting. I sometimes look down the list for any Keiths. They always prove to be well into their fifties. The only younger Keith I know of is Keith Lemon and I wonder if that is just his stage name. We Keiths are of our time.

★ ★ ★

One of the activities I always find difficult to understand is decorating the place with bunting. I hate bunting. I have now seen hundreds of different designs and colours of bunting, even knitted bunting. It would appear that people think that laughter, enjoyment and continual fun is bound to follow if bunting is hanging from trees or rafters. I just do not get it. It appears that some people think that a lovely glade of trees, under planted with beautiful flowers, can only be brought to life by hanging gaudy and garish pieces of cloth, cut in v shapes and attached by white, very visible string.

This bunting is usually hung by smiling staff who cannot help beaming because they, unlike me, love bunting. I have noticed that everyone who sees it remarks on the beauty of the bunting. Everyone that is, except that miserable Keith, who suffers from bunting phobia. Perhaps it was something that happened to me in my childhood. I sometimes wonder if all Keiths feel the same way. Maybe it's an age thing.

★ ★ ★

Another aspect of weddings at Crook Hall is that the guests have to find their way around a rather unusual site. This has sometimes presented problems. On one occasion a member of staff observed an elderly gentleman emerging from our coal shed and adjusting his clothing. He looked a little perturbed and muttered to our startled staff member that he appreciated that the building was old but he did think that the toilets needed some updating.

Our weddings usually take place in the Medieval Hall which has large fabric curtains hanging in the doorways. Our staff often hover behind the curtains when speeches or the ceremony are taking place, ready to assist with any last minute requests. At one of the weddings a guest was asked to switch off a light by the photographers. The guest obediently put his hand through the curtain to feel for the light switch. Unfortunately his groping fingers missed the switch and alighted upon the breast of our general manager. She stood shocked and motionless. She wondered what on earth was happening. The guest's hand continued to search around for the switch. Failing to find it, he popped his head through the curtain and was horrified to realise what he was holding. He apologised profusely. I think his embarrassment stayed with him for a good while.

★ ★ ★

Pricing is sometimes difficult. More than once we have found out we were selling something at a loss without even knowing. One week we needed champagne and forgot to order the required bottles. I had to pop out to buy some from a local supermarket. We ended up selling them at a loss.

I remember explaining our wedding pricing structure to the father of a bride to be. He was phoning in advance of coming to look at the Hall with his daughter. I recall the conversation almost verbatim;

I explained the cost of the venue hire.

He responded by saying, "'ow much?"

I repeated the price.

"Bloody 'ell," he retorted, "Does it include drinks?"

"No, that would be extra."

"Bloody 'ell, does it include food?"

"No, that would be extra as well."

"Bloody 'ell, you won't have many bookings will you?"

I informed him we were fully booked this year and almost booked up for next year. His predictable response was "Bloody 'ell."

The conversation finished and I was left with a vision of him discussing it with his family around the kitchen table. All of them saying in unison to each of his points,

"Bloody 'ell."

★ ★ ★

At one wedding I walked down to check the fires and I came across one of the bridesmaids who was in floods of tears.

I stopped and asked her, "Can I help in any way?"

She responded by saying, "No there is nothing you can do. There is nothing anyone can do. I am getting married in three weeks and…"

I wondered what was coming next, was she having second thoughts?

She went on to explain, "I am getting married somewhere else and now I have seen this I want to get married here."

Now that is the sort of feedback that makes you feel it is all worthwhile. I remember the words she uttered even if I can no longer picture her or which wedding she attended. Thank you, young lady. I certainly hope you had a wonderful wedding wherever it was held.

★ ★ ★

How romantic; organising an afternoon tea and proposing to the one you love over cakes and champagne. This was the plan when a young suitor booked a table, ordered a bottle of champagne and invited his loved one along. Everyone was made aware of the young man's plans. Every one that is, except the future fiancé. She did not accept. Indeed there appeared to be an argument after which she got up and left. On her way out our head waiter asked her if we would be seeing her again.

She shouted, "No but you might be seeing him again. With someone else."

What on earth had happened? Embarrassment all around.

★ ★ ★

A couple had booked the venue for their wedding. I was concerned when they did not contact us to plan their day. I rang them fearing that the wedding may have been cancelled.

The bride explained that there was just going to be the two of them, no guests, and asked if we could provide a witness and take some photographs. I was left wondering if this was an arranged marriage. When the day came it was an emotional, intimate ceremony. The couple then had a lovely afternoon tea in the gazebo followed by a stroll around the gardens. I was curious as to why they were on their own. They made no secret of this and were happy to tell me. They said that they had booked their wedding three times and each time one of their senior relatives could not make it. First time Auntie Madge and last time Uncle Timothy. They had had enough and decided they would never be able to please everyone so they decided to just go ahead in secret. Job done. I understood their situation.

★ ★ ★

Couples often leave items they no longer need after their wedding day. These range from table decorations to glasses and crockery and on one occasion bottles of lager. In this last case the couple had paid for more lager than they needed for the day. I think they had upwards of a 100 bottles left. I told them they were welcome to take the lager home. The groom had his eyes on the bottles and suggested that there would be plenty of space for them in their garage. The bride was adamant that we had to keep them; we could drink them, sell them or even throw them away but there was no way her new husband was going to have them in their garage. I think she had visions of him spending more time in the garage than in the house. In the first few weeks of marriage this was a non-starter. He looked very disappointed as she suggested that he should look on it as a tip to us for all our hard work. He looked resigned to the dry few weeks ahead of him.

★ ★ ★

We warn parents to keep an eye on their children because of dangers such as the very deep pond. However, the little ones sometimes get away from supervising parents. One boy got more than he bargained for when he sneaked up into our private quarters. Maggie had retired to bed early, leaving me to help the team downstairs. Suddenly she heard footsteps outside the bedroom door. Alarmed she leapt out of bed, not even stopping to put a dressing gown on over her white nightdress. When Maggie suddenly appeared in the shadowy hallway the young boy was terrified. He thought she was The White Lady. His reaction reminded Maggie of the young actor Macaulay Culkin in *Home Alone*. His jaw dropped in total amazement, his eyes opened to twice the size they should naturally be, and his arms shot up into the air. He screamed his head off. Maggie reached to take his arm and reassure him and said, "Where is your mother?" I am not sure what he heard as he let out a blood curdling yell and made a very sharp exit. He learnt a lesson that night – keep close to mum until you are sure of your surroundings. I think we may have lost a visitor to our Halloween events.

★ ★ ★

Running your own business can sometimes lead to conflict situations with others. No truer is this than with suppliers, especially wedding suppliers who have difficulty understanding who the customer is. They often have two – the couple and us. One such person set up some games which proved to be very popular with the guests. Maybe too popular. The lawn underneath was ruined. The supplier could not give a damn. I bore the cost of relaying the lawn but told him we would not have him or his business on the site again. Funnily enough two years later I spotted our newly appointed general manager, Nicola, sitting in the courtyard talking to this supplier. When I approached he did not seem to recognise me. I reminded him of our past discussions and then asked him to leave as I had not been joking the last time we met. Poor Nicola was a bit taken aback but understood when I later explained.

Thank goodness these incidents are few and far between. Our weddings have been a delight. We have really enjoyed sharing our house with all these happy couples and it is a privilege to be part of their celebrations. I tend to remember those events that are out of the ordinary but some of the sights have become more familiar; people enjoying themselves in the sunshine, having their wedding breakfast in the Medieval Hall, sipping champagne outside in the gardens, a bride and groom cutting their wedding cake under the apple tree. We did not realise that from these small beginnings we would go on to hold over eighty weddings a year. We have now hosted over 600 weddings in the Hall and the magic, romance and excitement never seem to fade.

★ ★ ★

One of our more recent weddings was that of our daughter. Her planning started with choosing a date. We broke the news to her that our calendar was booked up for two years. I cannot remember how the conversation went but the only availability was New Year's Eve. What a great choice! It was the best New Year's party I have ever attended. What's more it rolled over into a New Year's lunch in our new Garden Gate Café. Now both our children have been married at the Hall. What a joy.

9

EVENTS AND VISITS

Children love Crook Hall. They are enchanted as they wander around the gardens, exploring all the nooks and crannies. They are fascinated or scared by the ghosts, delighted with the wildlife and can have great fun running off all their energy doing the treasure hunts on event days or finding their way around the maze.

From a child's point of view the whole Crook Hall experience is a cross between *Puddle Lane* and *The Secret Garden*, with a smattering of other cherished children's adventure stories. We are very low tech so children can use their imagination and they find the place a source of fantasy. It is not a museum; it is a vibrant environment with families enjoying the atmosphere of the place. Maggie, with her background in education, was able to design activities and games the children would enjoy. She also organised the decorating of the tower rooms for our Fairy Tale event when Snow White, The Big Bad Wolf and Little Red Riding Hood take up residence. The events prove to be very popular and our staff, including myself, don costumes to entertain the children.

★ ★ ★

The first Easter we ran an event the temperature reached the upper eighties, almost unheard of at that time of year. I was the Easter Bunny and boy was that costume hot. I sweated as I had never sweated before. I swear I lost a stone in weight. People would have paid good money to do the workout I had that weekend, and the results showed as I had to literally tighten my belt on the Tuesday after the Bank Holiday Monday.

★ ★ ★

The following Easter was cooler. Against my better judgement Maggie persuaded me to don the rabbit suit and race around the gardens yet again. I was doing my best to bring passion to this important role of the 'Easter Bunny'. Difficult, because being pursued by over-enthusiastic children while dressed in a ridiculous costume of thick fur is not much fun. I made the mistake of going down to the entrance to the gardens. We were busy. Everyone seemed to be enjoying themselves and, on the face of it, even the grumpy man in the rabbit suit was joining in the fun.

Then disaster struck. Someone approached with a very large Alsatian. We do not normally let dogs into the garden but there was no stopping this one on seeing me in my costume. It launched itself, teeth first, through the gate. The growling snarls and open mouth were directed at the legs of this, by now, very timid, retiring white rabbit.

Some might say, "Oh well, the dog was scared."

This may well be true but not half as scared as I was. Only the quick thinking and brute strength of the owner prevented me from losing a bite sized chunk of leg. My leg! I beat a hasty retreat up the garden path trying to look cool and relaxed, an impossible task. The hound of the Baskerville's growls rang in my ears as I passed children clambering to be entertained. Forget that. I had my eyes firmly on an escape route. Once in the sanctuary of the Hall I retired upstairs to our private accommodation. I removed the head of the costume and looked in the mirror.

I had that 'just left the gym' look about me. What a carry on! Here I was, forty-five years old, dressed up as a bunny. What was I doing? Had it really come to this? I used to be an HR manager, working in a FTSE 500 company. I had run my own, very successful, management consultancy. And now? I was spending my weekend getting dressed up as a rabbit and being chased by Alsatians. Was I mad? Most probably.

★ ★ ★

At some events we have stories and games, and some children are invited to leave messages to The White Lady or wishes on the wishing tree. Whenever they come they can look for the troll under the bridge, the imps, the fairies or the grumpy gardener (the stone one not me) which are all hidden in and around the gardens.

★ ★ ★

Our Fairy Tale week is very important to us, and very appropriate. The wife of Dr Raine who lived here in the 1800s was Margaret Raine. She completed the first English translation of *Grimms' Fairy Tales*. One of our theatre groups, the Pantaloons, staged the play *The Brothers Grimm*. The Raines would have been pleased to have shared that evening, but, if you believe in ghosts, maybe they did.

When we first ran our Fairy Tale week we started on a small scale. My god-daughter, Jocelyn, took on the role of a fairy in the garden as well as working in the café along with our daughter Amanda and her friends. Mark (aka the bird man) seemed to be everywhere – moving tables, setting tables, serving people, washing up and also taking the part of The Big Bad Wolf.

The first day we were busy. All the scones went. The following day was incredible and we were even busier and we ran out of scones again. It seemed that the word in Durham was that Crook Hall was running a magical event.

By the last Sunday numbers had climbed beyond our wildest imaginings. It was now chaotically busy and we could not get the scones out fast enough. The systems we had set up on the first day were tested and strained to the limits. So too were our staff. Maggie discovered Mark lying in the turret dressed as the wolf, his legs in the air, his head in his hands and the wolf mask discarded beside him. He was sweating profusely and looked like a broken man rather than a scary wolf. He was genuinely exhausted. However, he was determined that the show would go on, so, groaning, he hauled himself to his feet, donned the mask and went back on stage with Little Red Riding Hood.

As we grew our business we began to recruit actors for some of these parts, much to the relief of our hard working staff. This was a great success. Our first professionally staffed event was our Alice in Wonderland Day. The Queen of Hearts chased the White Rabbit and Alice around the gardens with gusto. That evening one of the actors was recognised as Alice in the local Tesco by a group of youngsters who asked her for her autograph. She felt as if she had acquired celebrity status.

★ ★ ★

With all events, our approach was to start on a small scale and then wait to see if the event would catch the imagination of the public. Our 'Theatre in the Garden' events started slowly but then became one of the highlights of the year. The same could not be said for one of our favourite events. Candlelight Night. For this we lit the Hall and Gardens with over a thousand candles. Visitors were invited to wander through the candlelit woodland glades to the accompaniment of live music. We thought it was truly magical. However, every year we had poor turnouts. We would walk around the candlelit gardens after the visitors had left, enchanted, and think surely next year it will be a sell-out. No such luck. I think we ran it at a loss for six or seven years before reluctantly abandoning it. We could never persuade the public to see it in the same way as we viewed it. Disappointing but we had to ditch it.

★ ★ ★

The cacophony of the dawn chorus is a sound I always love. A real delight. We opened the Hall one morning at 5.20am and arranged for an expert from the RSPB to come along. He identified the sounds and pointed out the birds, telling us which bird was making which call. A fascinating nature trail.

Maggie made a cooked breakfast for everyone which was thoroughly enjoyed by all. Small beginnings indeed but far too early. I think we both enjoy our sleep too much to make it an annual event. If I wake early I sometimes wander around the garden enjoying the dawn chorus. A real joy, although I know that if I want to follow the stroll with a cooked breakfast I will be the one doing the cooking.

★ ★ ★

As a part time bit-actor with a CV which extended to playing the Easter Bunny, I was persuaded to take on the role of the ghost – much against my better judgement. Although, now I come to think about it, I was in some ways taking on my natural role – appearing when summoned by Maggie. At Halloween, Maggie would tell ghost tales to all the visitors standing near the moat pool. The tales would culminate in a story about The White Lady and her appearance across the field. The children would ring a bell which they were told summoned The White Lady. So on the third ring, to the accompaniment of much shouting and screaming, I would emerge in costume from the woods at the other side of the field. A well trained ghost. One year there were horses in the field which added to the spectacle. As I stood up to scare fellow humans the equine audience reared up and galloped across the field. I felt as if I had supernatural powers and so did the audience. They were enthralled and thought the horses were all part of the show.

Earlier, as I had been getting ready for my appearance by climbing into the costume in the public wood, I had terrified two anglers who were walking along to the fish ponds which lay deeper in the woods. Their horrified faces were a treat to see, but I took my hood off to reassure them.

The tables were turned the following year when a ferocious Rottweiler, rather than two anglers, confronted me. So, on that occasion I was the one who was terrified. Fortunately the dog's owner had two hands on the leash and kept the growling animal at bay. Without those steady hands I would have been off over the field pursued by an angry canine. No doubt it would have led to hilarity from the onlookers who had come to be frightened rather than humorously entertained.

★ ★ ★

Our first Christmas event was very low key with just a few visitors and we had to keep on waking Father Christmas up to greet the children. The coal fire had just been far too cosy for our Santa and he was continually nodding off and snoring. His grotto was in one of the smaller rooms next to the kitchen and as the popularity of the event increased over subsequent years a bigger room was required. We now have the grotto in the tower room, and with scheduled appointments, so that we have a clear idea of how many people will be visiting. No time now for a napping Father Christmas. We are always fully booked.

I remember an incident in those early days when panic spread through the Laplanders as Santa had run out of presents. The last visitor, a young boy called Sam, was destined to have no gift. A quick thinking elf, aka Maggie, ran upstairs to our private accommodation and took one of our children's presents from under our tree. Sam went home with a lovely present and Ian still does not know that he was a present down that year.

A treasure hunt is organised for all our events and Christmas is no exception. We have a hidden clue in each garden and there is a small prize for all the children who successfully complete the hunt. For some inexplicable reason one little girl thought she was going to be rewarded with a real live kitten. She was very disappointed when she was handed a small candy bar.

Some of the interactions with Father Christmas have been memorable; the young boy who came in and fell to his knees praying as if the man in the red suit was a messiah. Another boy, when placed on one of the small seats, had his feet firmly facing the exit so he could run out as soon as he got his present. One boy asked if he could have a private consultation with Father Christmas in order to report that he was being bullied. He hoped Santa could make the torment stop. That one touched my heart.

Nearly all the children are looking for rather more material presents from Father Christmas. They usually have a fairly fixed idea of the toy they want. One youngster brought out three sheets of foolscap and started to reel off his requirements. It sounded like the inventory of Hamleys. Father Christmas had to let him down gently by pointing out that he only had one sleigh.

We have information about each child on booking so Father Christmas is always well briefed about the children who are scheduled in to see him. In one instance a six year old boy called Joshua came along. Father Christmas had been told that it was Joshua's seventh birthday the next day and he had a dog called Rocky. Joshua came in with two of his siblings and a cousin.

He inspected Santa carefully before asking suspiciously "Are you the real Father Christmas?"

Santa responded by asking "Are you the real Joshua? Is it your birthday tomorrow? And will you be taking your dog Rocky for a walk?"

There was complete silence as Joshua's eyes grew almost to the size of plates and his jaw dropped. He remained silent for the rest of the interchange. He was entranced.

Sometimes there have been embarrassing moments for the adults. Father Christmas always asked the children whether grown up family members had been good.

On one occasion a young boy replied, "Yes Mum has been good but Dad has been very naughty."

"What makes you think Dad has been so naughty?" enquired Father Christmas.

"Because Mum says so. She says he is so naughty that he has to sleep in the spare room."

Mum added grimly that he would be remaining there until he began to behave better. Toes were curling. Too much information. Father Christmas moved swiftly on.

★ ★ ★

People sometimes leave some of their belongings at the Hall. I usually wander around the gardens after we are closed just checking that all the gates are shut. One evening I thought all my birthdays had come at once when I almost tripped over a large wad of cash – rolled up twenty pound notes. I was most excited. I knew that I would have to hand it in at the police station, but I also knew that if it was not claimed I would be able to keep it. Unfortunately for me the owner rang ten minutes later to ask if we had found any cash in the gardens. My disappointment was matched by his delight when I said I had found it. Some of the older readers may remember Lorraine Chase of 'Luton Airport' fame. We found her purse in the Hall. Fortunately for her I am old enough to remember her persona and was able to trace her and return her credit cards, currency etc.

One woman left a very pretty ring in one of the bathrooms. Maggie found it and popped it on her finger for safe keeping. A couple of hours later she and Nicola were having a wedding planning meeting with a bride and her mother. The bride's mother asked if an eternity ring had been handed in. Maggie was most embarrassed and wished the ground would swallow her up as she flashed her hand at the woman and asked if this was the lost ring. Nicola pointed out that looking after lost rings was a very important job at Crook Hall. Everyone laughed as the ring was returned to the rightful finger.

★ ★ ★

Throughout the year we welcome lots of coach trips and sometimes there are passengers who have mobility issues. One such trip is indelibly imprinted on my memory. A very thoughtful coach driver had arrived with five mobility scooters on board for the use of his elderly passengers. Unfortunately, he assumed riding a mobility scooter was a universal skill. Such an assumption was poorly grounded as were the first drivers arriving at the gates. Five mobility scooters hit the garden led by a Lewis Hamilton-like character who was definitely in pole position. Well, that was until they hit the first corner at high speed. They crashed into each other and one of the drivers was thrown off.

She sprawled on the grass and shouted at the top of her voice "GET ENID! GET ENID."

I imagined Enid arriving in some sort of support vehicle. Instead an elderly woman strode around the corner like some Matron from a pre-1970 sitcom.

"Thank goodness you are here," one of them called to her, "Maureen's badly hurt."

Enid was not sympathetic. She pulled the woman to

her feet, brushed her down and marched her off into the gardens. I heard her admonishing her charge for being far too mobile to need one of those scooters and besides they were death-traps.

I was left to push, rather than ride, the scooters back to the bus. Seeing the crash site the coach driver was now interviewing the passengers as to whether they knew how to drive the scooters. Those who had fallen off were exchanging tales of their near death experiences.

* * *

I am always amazed by how many people present fiction as fact. On numerous occasions I have been firmly told that Crook Hall is a National Trust property and that we are 'in the book'. This is usually propounded by people who have the card in their hands and no book.

One particular dad, on being told that under threes could get in free, introduced his son as a three year old. The indignant young boy chirped up that he was five next week – much to dad's embarrassment. Indeed he was so embarrassed that he offered to do the washing up.

One day we had a very special visitor. This was Olwyn Ratcliffe who had been an evacuee during the war. She was very excited to be back in Durham and told us that she and her younger brother John had fallen on their feet when they were evacuated from the Blitz to Crook Hall. She told us of the kindness of the owners, Mr and Mrs Cassels, who had been incredible and they had felt so welcomed by the wider Durham community. Her main memories were of the site being right on the edge of the town with the countryside behind. She also had a few stories to tell about the ghost. It was lovely to know that things had not changed.

The majority of our visitors are absolutely lovely and we have been delighted to welcome them into our home. Our lives have been enriched by our contact with them. They come from countries all over the world, places as far flung as Tasmania, Uzbekistan and Mongolia to name just a few.

★ ★ ★

As I say most visitors are very pleasant but sometimes we get an exception and then I try to bite my tongue and keep my own counsel but I don't always succeed.

If I was at the entrance and anyone was rude I refused them entry. Sometimes in a rather Basil Fawlty sort of way. One young woman approached the gate on a very busy bank holiday. She demanded free entry for herself, her mother and a few others in her party to discuss the prospect of using the premises as her wedding venue. I informed her that this was not possible but we could fix an appointment for another day. She could of course pay to have a look around today, however, she would not be able to meet with any staff member to discuss her wedding as it was too busy. She became quite insistent. As did I. Then she said she did not like my attitude. I told her I was less than keen on hers. She then announced to me and her family that this might not be the right place for her wedding. I voiced my agreement with her conclusion. This did not go down well. She stormed off, shouting over her shoulder that she intended to write a letter of complaint to the owner.

"Good luck with that," I responded.

On another occasion I was met by a very rude person who had a group of walkers with her. They hovered some distance away, possibly fearful of the wrath she was about to let loose on me. She was insistent that she and her party could come in for free to have a coffee. She told me she had been informed of this by someone she had met in town. I told her this was not possible. She then tried to give me a rational business case as to why free access should be given to these very thirsty coffee drinkers. I was adamant. I explained to her we had plans to build a café at the entrance which would be open to all, but, at the moment, if they wanted to visit our café in the Hall then an entrance charge would be required. She kept on going back to her group to report the progress of the negotiations. She finally came back and crossly informed me that she would never come here again. To my shame I sarcastically pointed out that this was not possible as she had never been here once. She marched off leading her compliant group away, muttering that the unpleasant man on the entrance gate must think he owns the place.

We were not open every day and on occasion people appeared on days we were advertised as closed. Some people persisted in trying to gain access, coming up the private lane. Maggie, forever the diplomat, dealt with most of these people with sympathy and politeness. However, one day a woman was particularly angry that we were closed. Maggie said the woman was very aggressive and rude. She shouted such abuse that in the end Maggie let her know in a very calm voice that she would not be welcome even when we were open. I sometimes wish I could be calm and collected in such situations. I tend to lose it.

★ ★ ★

A woman who lived in England emailed complaining about a visit which she had made with her mother-in-law. She claimed that her mother-in-law, who was visiting from Africa, had not enjoyed her visit. I had to send a reply to her pointing out that her mother-in-law had indeed loved her visit and her comments in our visitor book attested to this. I enclosed a scanned entry of her mother-in-law's comments.

'What a beautiful place. Thank you for a wonderful day. I am visiting my son and daughter-in-law and this has been a highlight of the trip.'

She had signed her comments and left her African address.

Maybe the complainant was stressed by having her mother-in-law staying with her. You just never know what is going on in people's lives.

I sometimes struggle to understand what people are thinking. I served a table of four elderly women and a retired man. He insisted he would tip the waiter and the women all thanked him for his generosity. I less than gratefully accepted the 2p he put in the tip jar.

One thing that people are very generous with is advice. One person, on an especially busy day, suggested that we should run a bed and breakfast. I thanked her for the suggestion but it left me muttering crossly to myself.

I am busy trying to get a life. I certainly do not need any more activities to manage. People sleeping in our beds at night? Over my dead body.

Others would suggest that we should do some marketing to let people know we are open. Most irritating when the comments follow a week when we have had some national press coverage or have been on television.

We have also had some visitors suggesting that we need more signage around the city – as if we have some magic wand and a wave is all it takes. These visitors are always surprised when we let them know that we have paid for many of the white on brown signs. And they do not come cheap.

However, these customers, although frustrating, are nothing compared to the people who look down their noses at you and treat you as a second class citizen or worse. That is, they do, until they discover that you own the place. They then metamorphose into fawning fools. Thankfully, these people are fairly rare. Maggie and I have no time for them.

One Easter we estimated we would have about 350 visitors and knew we would be busy. 600 arrived and we struggled to cope. We then had some poor feedback saying there were not enough chairs, that people had to wait for tables, and that it was chaotic and poorly managed. The feedback was valid. That particular Easter led me to sit back and once again reassess our position.

"Why do we bother?" I asked Maggie. "We do not need to do this. We do not have to share the place with anyone else."

Then I thought of all our staff who had worked alongside us to build up the business and the wonderful feedback we usually receive. I quickly dismissed those negative thoughts.

* * *

When we do receive poor feedback, and I am pleased to say it is only occasionally, I always respond. One visitor wrote in saying that she had met an old man in the garden (that was me). She had asked him what a particular plant was and he told her what it was (and I was right) but the lady wrote that the scruffy old man did not look as if he knew what he was talking about. On that occasion I enjoyed writing a reply peppered with Latin plant names – from the old man in the garden.

Apart from these isolated examples most of our visitors are delightful people who we are pleased to welcome into our home.

* * *

We have always encouraged groups to visit us and Maggie is adept at welcoming them and making them feel at home. I used to help serving teas and scones but rarely spent any time with them. All this changed when Maggie and Amanda organised a long weekend in New York. It seemed such a good idea at the time and I actively encouraged Maggie to go.

While she was away a volcano erupted in Iceland and spewed an ash cloud across the whole northern hemisphere. This huge ash cloud grounded all aircraft across Europe and North America, so Maggie and Amanda were stranded in New York for nearly two weeks. One of the groups booked in over her extended absence had ordered baked potatoes. This was the first time we had served hot potatoes and the first time I had cooked one, let alone forty-eight.

The group were due at twelve noon and I was in the kitchen by seven. I was feverishly reading Delia Smith's page on baked potatoes. I do not think I had read a page of text so often since I was at school attempting to decipher a French translation. At least I understood the content this time but the stress levels felt very similar. Delia suggested what you should do with four potatoes, and I had over forty sitting on a table in front of me. I reassured myself that it was just a question of scale. Then I looked at the small door of the Aga. They would not all fit in that little space. I cursed the ash cloud. It did not help. I then thought I would cook them in batches. I had time on my side and by 9.30 the staff would arrive.

Fortunately for me and our visitors one of the staff saw that I was floundering and took control. Within seconds we had a process established and things went swimmingly. Everyone enjoyed their baked potatoes.

The weeks Maggie was 'trapped' in New York on an extended holiday I was extending myself in a quick induction into all the duties Maggie usually undertook. What hard work. All the team, but especially me, were pleased to see her return so that normal service could be resumed.

Having said that, I had a wonderful time working in

the kitchen. There was a great team spirit. One of the young girls asked where ham came from. Mark quickly piped up,

"It comes from an animal called a ham."

This was accepted without question. He added that it gets its name from the noise it makes and he demonstrated by making a very deep resounding,

"Hammmm hammmm."

He sounded like a panellist from that old show *Call My Bluff*. His bluff was not called by the girl in question and for months afterwards the sound of this mythical beast was heard every time anyone put a ham sandwich into a toasting machine. It took the poor girl quite a while to live that one down.

Our scones had always been an attraction for our visitors but they were not the only choice on the menu. Our toasties were made to be as tasty as the best we had ever had elsewhere. Top of the requirements was good quality cheese with an excellent flavour. I spent a number of days over one summer in my role of quality inspector randomly choosing and eating a cheese toasty, ensuring the right quantity of cheese was in the right type of bread and that it was toasted to the right level. By the end of the season the offering was perfect and my waistband was wider. Some of our season ticket holders came back drawn by our toasties along with our other culinary delights.

A new member joined our catering team. She was in her twenties, slim and attractive and had excellent interpersonal skills. She did a splendid job for a few years. She also developed a passion for our cheese toasties, she had them for lunch every day. I was reminded of Renée Zellweger. Apparently the actress drank a pint of beer and ate a pizza each day to hit her target weight for her role in the film *Bridget Jones's Diary*. Our waitress had no such role but she loved her toasted sandwich lunches to the point that she bought her own toasty machine and ingredients so she could eat the same toasties on her day off. Her weight began to balloon. She finally left. We all thought she had been to a clinic for her addiction to cheese toasties. Our imagination ran wild.

We fantasised about her standing up in the circle and saying," My name is Sandy and I am a cheese toasty addict. It all began at Crook Hall…'

Anyway, she had left and I do hope she has regained the pleasure of an occasional cheese toasty and a weight she is happy with.

One of the skills I really appreciate in the kitchen is creativity. For five years we served a soup of the day. It was always carrot and coriander which was delicious but took a long time to make. One day there was an incredible run on the soup. Everyone seemed to want a bowl even though it was a warm day. The fickleness of customers knows no bounds. There was a sudden desperate need to find some more soup. We did not have enough time to make another batch. Speed was imperative. I was frantically pulling cans from our kitchen cupboards, waving them at Nicola and asking,"Can you do anything with this?"

She rejected the tuna in brine, the baked beans and sausages, the chilli beans. Then I struck gold. Some tins of tomatoes hiding in the back of the cupboard. Had we any basil? We looked through the spice cupboard finding all sorts of old favourites used once and then forgotten. Then I remembered we had some basil in the greenhouse. Oh, and the order was given to bring an onion and some garlic from the vegetable patch.

Nicola ended up making some lovely tomato and basil soup and that was the move away from carrot and coriander being served every day. Now we serve a wide range of soups and one of the favourites is tomato and basil, based on a recipe Nicola invented under extreme pressure. Genius.

★ ★ ★

We are keen to welcome people with mobility issues and we are happy to push their wheelchairs. The historical layout provides many challenges, especially the steep slope at the entrance to the gardens which makes even the physically fit puff a little. I found out that the land falls 300 metres from the railway line to the river. No wonder that Durham is sometimes described as the city of hills.

The oldest person to visit was 105 and she used a wheelchair. I pushed her round all the accessible areas and she and her daughter had a thoroughly enjoyable time.

Another wheelchair user was a young man who I would have believed to be Paralympian given the speed with which he shot around the gardens; no help was requested and no help was needed.

On one occasion, I remember taking over the

wheelchair pushing duties from a husband who was struggling. His rather large wife feebly told me that she was very ill. I pushed, shoved and sweated and finally got our infirm visitor up to the seating area just outside the office and then I was off to see to some other issue. On returning I found that the chair was empty. I looked around for the missing invalid, only to be told that she had gone for a walk around the garden. Eventually, I found her wandering unaided around the Medieval Hall. Hmmmm. Was it a miracle? I felt as if I was in a scene from *Little Britain*.

10

BUILDING FOR THE FUTURE

We attended a local council meeting where we listened to the head of tourism referring to Crook Hall as a great place for children's events. This was a pivotal moment for our business. I remember returning home that night and discussing the implications of this point with Maggie.

We agreed that if we wanted to grow our business then we needed to be seen as more than just a venue for children's events. If we continued with such a narrow focus then we were open to competition from many similar operations who cater solely for children. We had to stand out from the crowd. We had to clearly identify what made Crook Hall different. Our buildings and gardens are our unique selling point. The Hall and Gardens are the things which cannot be replicated. There are plenty of excellent children's activity centres in the North East but only one Medieval Hall surrounded by gardens.

One of our challenges has always been to make

Crook Hall a place which attracts visitors all year round. With a tourist attraction based around a garden we had to think very carefully as to how to extend the season. When it rained or the weather was poor we still needed visitors. We knew the answer lay in making the indoor space more interesting and offering more pre-bookable events. This would mean people would visit irrespective of the weather.

Our first plan was to expand our very popular family Christmas events. We decided to open in the early evening for carols, mince pies, mulled wine and a visit to Father Christmas. This was aimed at adults who would enjoy seeing the Hall and Gardens decorated for Christmas, but who did not necessarily have children to bring. We first marketed it as 'An Adult's Christmas' but quickly changed this title when we received some very strange phone calls!

Caller; "I would like to book a ticket for your adult Christmas."

Maggie; "Certainly, which evening would you prefer?"

Caller; "What would you suggest? Are some of the evenings raunchier than others?"

Maggie; "I beg your pardon!"

Once the misunderstanding about the title had been cleared up the event was a huge success, with some of our older guests visiting Father Christmas for the first time in their lives.

The following summer we turned our attention to our afternoon teas. We had begun to serve these in the gardens but as they grew in popularity we found we needed more indoor seating when the weather was poor.

Nicola, our dynamic new manager, suggested using our private drawing room as an alternative seating area on rainy days. This was destined to be a phenomenal success.

The beautiful room had views across the gardens to the castle and Cathedral. What a superb alternative to sitting in the gardens. It was possibly one of the best views in Durham. It was the view which had blown us away on our first visit to the Hall. Nicola persuaded us to move our living quarters to the second floor and leave the whole of the first floor to our visitors. She was convinced we would fill the rooms with afternoon tea bookings. She was to be proved correct. Moreover, we were able to extend the serving of afternoon teas throughout the year.

At the same time we were looking to recruit some permanent professional staff to support Nicola in running the business. The days of ourselves, helped by a team of students running the place, were over.

★ ★ ★

By 2014, we realised that our catering facilities could not cope with the increasing numbers of visitors. The demand for afternoon teas was rocketing and our domestic kitchen lacked the space to continue to provide a quality job. We began to have serious service problems. On some Sundays we were serving over fifty afternoon teas and upwards of 200 other people were wanting refreshments from our café. We were pushing the limits of our capacity.

In addition we had an entrance shed which, while

quirky, did not reflect the quality of what we were offering. The shed had no heating or lighting. We were now open all year round. The autumn and winter shifts could prove to be very cold and wet for the person working at the entrance. This was usually Dorothy, one of Maggie's friends, who volunteers with us. She was stoic, turning up in her ski gear, and bringing hot water bottles and blankets to help her through the long cold afternoons. If I expressed concerns about the cold to Dorothy, she would assure me that there was no such thing as poor weather just poor clothing. What a trooper!

We hatched a plan to provide a heater and lighting in the shed but after numerous discussions our plan evolved into a visitor centre with an apartment above. Mission Creep. I had interviewed a number of potential architects, but few really understood what we wanted. We finally offered the architectural brief to a young woman from Hexham.

The apartment was essential to the scheme. We had to generate some cash to help to pay for the loan. As we were privately owned I knew that there would be no grants or lottery funding available to help with the scheme. We were on our own. The loan was huge and, unlike other schemes we had embarked upon, this investment was desirable but not essential.

Lyndsey, our architect, was totally in tune with us. She created and designed a truly remarkable building, a building of its time which represented our green credentials but also reflected the wood, stone and brick materials which already existed in the fabric of Crook Hall. The high pitched roof and the outdoor space was all in keeping with the experience of visiting the Hall and Gardens.

As one of our young staff remarked, "It is totally modern but with a Crook Hall twist."

I was not surprised when it won two awards from the Royal Institute of British Architects.

Lindsay managed the project within budget and within the tight timescale. The ground was broken in the September and we were serving the first customers by the beginning of April the following year.

The only organisation not to meet the deadline was Openreach. What a disaster they were. We had dug all the trenches for the utilities to be connected including the telephones. All the connections were to be well hidden in order to emphasise the straight clear lines of the building.

The Openreach engineer arrived on the allotted day and, after much humming and harring, informed us that he was the wrong engineer and BT would get back to us.

We waited and waited and despite many phone calls we continued to wait. Once the build was complete and the concrete and paving in place, they turned up unannounced. They informed us that we needed to dig a trench. We told them that we had just filled in the trench that we had dug for them five weeks earlier. They suggested that their preferred option was to bring in an overhead line. The lead engineer said the overhead cable would be fine; it could be attached to the apex of the building and tracked down the middle of the gable end. I thought he was joking then I saw his face and realised he was deadly serious. I looked at him in total disbelief.

We had worked so hard with the architect and builders in making a building which was attractive and with clean lines. This man wanted to put a line right through it. Unbelievable.

I sent him packing. He left with his cable between his legs.

A real disappointment.

We had an alternative phone from Vodafone within twenty-four hours but getting wi-fi took longer and was fraught with difficulties. However, it is now in place and all without the 'help' of Openreach. Thank goodness.

Apart from this, the build was a great success and we were all delighted. The holiday apartment is very popular and is booked up for most of the year. I am so pleased I did not follow the advice of many people who suggested we could put four student units into the space. That might have made us more money but the holiday let fits our business.

★ ★ ★

The new café, The Garden Gate, has not been without its teething problems. The business had taken a new direction. We did not realise that dealing with a visitor who was viewing the Hall and Gardens and wanted a quick drink or a bite to eat was quite different to those who were coming with a primary need to visit a café. This took some adjustment on our part.

We had imagined that people would pop in for coffee and cake but found that lots of customers wanted lunch. There was very little preparation space and it was a real challenge for the team. We reorganised the workspace and put in some extra shelving. These days the staff work wonders, whipping up delicious soups, sandwiches and mezes as well as the cakes and scones for which we are famous. I do not know how they do it.

I was particularly excited about my plan for the background music in the café. I wanted to play vinyl on my inherited Ferguson radiogram. The radiogram had been bought by my parents when they were newly married and had been in their RAF married quarters all round the world. Now it was back in the North East, less than five miles from Spennymoor where it was originally manufactured. I was also keen to start with the first record I had ever owned. So the first cafetiere coffee served in The Garden Gate was accompanied by strains of Marianne Faithful singing 'Summer Nights'. She was singing about magic, little cafés, romance. Perfect.

I loved it but both the cafetieres and the music proved to be equally unpopular with the visitors. We replaced the cafetieres with a coffee machine and my cherished radiogram with a CD player. Well, if I have learnt anything in these twenty years it is you just have to follow the market. Good coffee? Good music? The arbiter is the customer not a grumpy old man who listens to old music on old record players. Never mind. I clearly know what I like as I return to my flat with my cafetiere coffee and my turntable, and, in the safety of my retreat, forget the customer and sing along to my music. Perfect.

★ ★ ★

Nicola started using jam jars for our soft drinks and water. Evidently it was the new trend and we were already using them for cocktails at some of our weddings. Maggie and I thought it was a dreadful idea but what do we know? Nicola often has to press us to add a modern twist or adjust to a new trend.

Maggie asked a few customers what they thought of this jam jar idea. A well-spoken elderly visitor from the south expressed some reservations but added sympathetically,"Never mind. I know you are poor in the north."

★ ★ ★

At the same time this project was going on we had our favourite builders, Derek and Dan Petrie, making some changes in the main building. They were assisting us in our move up to the third floor of the Georgian house. Our new, smaller living space was ideal for the two of us. Even this did not come without its trials and tribulations. A ceiling collapse, rotten floorboards to repair and wood wormed beams to treat.

The ceiling collapse led us to have to clear a good deal of rubbish out of the windows on the third floor. We were throwing rubble, plaster and wood out into the gardens. We had one of our staff members help. The person we chose to help was a well-built Durham undergraduate who hailed from the south. Language proved to be a barrier. In this case one of the builders gave out an instruction to our undergraduate in a dialect our student had never heard before.

"Gan o'er er and hoy oot the clart and tat."

Our Durham student lowered his head closer to the smaller guy who had given this command and said very slowly and clearly, "I am sorry but I do not understand a word that you have spoken."

I was there to offer a quick translation.

"He has asked you to go over to the window and throw the rubbish out into the garden."

He nodded and was onto the task immediately thinking it best to ask no more questions. I wish he had asked a few clarifying questions because his view of rubbish was somewhat different than mine. Fortunately I was just in time to stop him from throwing a very heavy radiator out of the window. If it had landed on the guy working below in the gardens it would have killed him.

By the end of the shift these two 'foreigners' had developed a mutual respect for each other but communication between them was carried out in a very tentative manner.

This story had echoes of our daughter Amanda's first weeks at Bristol University where some fellow students could not understand her North East accent and asked her which country she came from.

There certainly is a north-south divide.

★ ★ ★

In the Georgian house smoke from the chimneys was causing problems. We had open fires on every floor as we believed coal fires added to the ambience of the place. The loft was full of smoke, and on some days it was seeping out into the bedrooms.

Our first step was to plaster the internal gable end of the attic where we thought the smoke was coming from. This failed to resolve the problem. Although the attic became smoke free, smoke was now appearing in all the top rooms. We then tried blocking up the fireplace on the top floor. This cleared that room but sent the smoke down two floors into the dining room. We therefore had the dining room flue lined. A success. The dining room was now smoke free for the first time in years. I was delighted until I saw the smoke bellowing down the stairs from the first floor drawing room. Back to the drawing board.

The experts suggested we needed to line two more flues. I questioned this, thinking of the expense. They invited me to have a look down the chimney for myself. I would need to go up on a cherry picker and, being scared of heights, this was not something I was keen to do. Nevertheless, I clambered on board and with shaking legs I was hoisted up to the top of the chimney. Clinging on for grim life, I peered down into the cavity of the chimney. It was bad news. As the builder had explained, all the feathers (that is the bricks between each chimney flue to you and me) had completely disintegrated. We did need both chimneys lined in order to stop the smoke. We just had to find the money.

Thus, the beginning of 2015 was a very sooty, cold, dusty and expensive three months for the two of us. We were living in one room in the top of the building, in the garret I had used as a paint room when we had first arrived twenty years earlier. All our prized possessions and our clothes were under dust sheets. The heating was not working. We felt like students again. Impoverished students at that. Spirits were low.

By April all was sorted. The building work was complete. We had warm, clean accommodation. Moreover, we could gaze out of our refurbished living area and see the newly completed café at the bottom of the meadow.

We turned to each other and chorused with feeling, "The last major building project we are ever doing."

Now all we had to do was to generate enough cash to pay for it.

★ ★ ★

While we have metaphorically moved above the shop we are still keen to keep the place as close to a family home as possible. When we have friends round, provided there is no function on, we have a choice of rooms to use. We still have dinner parties in the Medieval Hall or the dining room. It is good to know the house is still used as intended when it was designed and built. Feasts and celebrations have brought people together in this house for centuries. When sharing an evening with friends I sometimes look around the table and wonder who has sat here before us in times long gone and what were they celebrating?

11

OUR TEAM

Our staff have been fantastic. We have always been fortunate in having a group of people who have not only worked hard, but have also bought into Crook Hall's ethos; every visitor is treated as a friend you would welcome into your own home. There have been some staff members, it's fair to say, who have not made the grade but I usually felt they were lovely people who happened to find themselves in the wrong job.

One of our students was continually arriving late for work. It culminated in him arriving half an hour late, dressed in the same clothes that he had left in the previous evening. Hmmm… He looked tired out and we suspected he had been out all night. He blamed his lateness on the trains. Kelly, our general manager invited him into the office. He knew what was going to happen.

Kelly, "Please would you come in to the office?"

Student; "Don't want to."

Kelly, rather more forcibly, "Come into the office."

The student shuffled in through the door.

Kelly, "Please take a seat."

Student, "Don't want to."

Kelly, exasperated, "Take a seat."

Student, "It's OK I know what you are going to say and I do not want to work here anyway."

A case of jumping before he was pushed.

Kelly is often called upon to deal with challenging situations. One evening she was overseeing a wedding when the staff alerted her to a drunken intruder who was stumbling around the gardens. The man could barely stand. He was getting alarmingly close to the moat pool. She tried to persuade him to leave. He was having none of it. She was worried that he could fall into the water.

Kelly's partner is a member of the local police force so, in desperation, she rang him. He was on duty and Kelly began to explain the situation. Suddenly the man stepped towards the moat pool and teetered on the edge of the water. Kelly, though petite, is very brave. She rushed forward to save him, dropping her phone in the process. Her partner, fearing the worst, burst into action. Within five minutes four police cars arrived. They entered the premises like a SWAT team. Within minutes everything was sorted and the uninvited guest was helped off the premises. I wonder what he remembered of the incident when he woke up the following morning.

★ ★ ★

We always aim to be five-star in everything we do and we know if someone cannot give a five-star service we cannot continue to employ them. Maintaining our reputation for excellent service is sacrosanct.

Input from our customers has been vital in helping us to operate at this level. We always welcome feedback. When we do fail to reach the expected standards we are all disappointed. We try never to promise things we cannot deliver.

Some people, like Beth and Georgia, started working here when they were fifteen and are still with us. Georgia works during her holidays from university, while Beth is now one of our senior managers. Three of Georgia's sisters have worked here. We are a family affair. Gary, one of our team, has frequently been asked whether he is my son and during one exchange was given a hearty handshake and congratulated on the fine work he has done in opening the Hall and Gardens. He acknowledged the compliment, adding that he had found it all extremely hard work. He says that all these comments about his parentage have sometimes led him to go home questioning his own identity.

Mark was an extremely flexible member of the team. He came back from college one Easter and helped me move a few logs. At least I think that is how I sold the task to him. Our tree surgeon had brought down the sycamores surrounding the Silver and White Garden. He had logged the trees and left half the orchard filled with timber. I had never seen so many logs. Neither had Mark.

Three days later we slumped against an apple tree completely exhausted but triumphant. The logs were now all neatly stacked in the log store near the house. I could see from Mark's face that he preferred moving tables and chairs for weddings to moving logs, but he never complained. We congratulated each other on an amazing log pile that would keep the fires going for many seasons. I think we still have some left.

We have had some great staff whose devotion to the cause has taken my breath away. Biddy, who came from Worcester, graduated from Durham University but travelled all the way back the following October to be our witch at Halloween – she had so enjoyed the role the previous year. She was such a good actor. Superb.

Hannah, another student at the university, played a pivotal role in the early years when our wedding business began. She, too, demonstrated total commitment: she had to travel home to Edinburgh one Friday evening after work to visit a sick relative. She spent the whole night sitting at a hospital bedside but she was back at the Hall to manage a wedding the following morning at 8am. She was a very talented singer and graced the stage at many of our events, including our candlelight nights, and returned after graduation to sing again. What a star she was.

Since leaving, Hannah has gone on to be a professional singer and actress, she is incredibly talented.

Look her up. Hannah Howie.

James, one of our current students, is 'Mr Flexible'. He has been a waiter and barman but has also excelled as an actor. Each day I see him he seems to be in a different outfit; elf, army officer, pirate, bunny rabbit, snowman, Prince Charming, big bad wolf. You name it, give him a costume and he is away. No role except those more feminine ones are beyond him. He is such a good sport and he is very good with all the children.

It seems that every year the university provides us with some excellent staff.

Some of our staff have had embarrassing experiences. One of our young lads, Jack, was working at a twenty-first party one evening when he spilt a quantity of prosecco down the front of his shirt. Unbeknown to us he called his father, who arrived at the Hall with a new shirt. Jack swapped shirts in the car park and rushed back to work. One of the guests arrived late, saw him bare chested in the car park and thought he was a stripper. An excited ripple went through the Hall when this news was reported to her friends. There was disappointment when Jack's clothes stayed on him for the rest of the evening. The buttons were tightly fastened.

★ ★ ★

Malcolm worked with us as a gardener for many years. It's thanks to him that I was introduced to the beauty of the camellia and his knowledge of hydrangeas has made such a difference to the gardens. He re-laid the brick paths in the Shakespeare Garden making them more symmetrical and more in keeping with the period.

We had no shortage of bricks. In the 1800s and early 1900s the Durham Brick and Tile Company was operating in close proximity to the Hall. Nearly all the larger towns had their own brick making facilities. Durham was not alone. Bricks were manufactured in their millions to provide building materials for the thousands of back to back housing and finer dwellings which were springing up all around the county.

Once the Brick and Tile Company closed, probably due to foreign competition from Mackems or Geordies, the bricks were just left in the ground in and around the old site. We have salvaged hundreds of them and to our delight discovered three bricks which have Crook Hall printed on the end. These special bricks were made to identify the recipient of each particular production batch. I gave one of these bricks to the gardener and asked him to put it in the wall just outside the courtyard so our visitors could see it. Fortunately the cement was still wet when I discovered he had put it in the wrong way round so that the Crook Hall name was not visible.

An advert for Specsavers, I thought.

More recently we found local bricks stamped with the names of the brickworks where they had been produced, such as Lumley and Newburn and we have used them to make an interesting edging around the gravelled area.

★ ★ ★

We have a vine in the greenhouse. It was the one we brought with us from our previous home. One year we took off thirty kilos of grapes and turned them into wine. We had special bottles made. The alcohol was there, the colour was there, the bottles certainly looked good. The taste? What a disappointment. Maggie actually spat out her first mouthful. I laid a few bottles down – for ever. It was a bad vintage. No other years were planned. On reflection I do feel the colour is very reminiscent of the paraffin my dad used to use in our old heater.

★ ★ ★

John joined us to work in the gardens a few years after Malcolm started. John is a devoted Manchester United fan. For many seasons he travelled down to Old Trafford to see the good games as well as the bad ones. He did not renew his season ticket once Ferguson left or was it because there were more poor games than good ones?

In the garden, he transformed the scruffy vegetable patch into a well organised kitchen garden and he has added to the autumn colours by introducing dahlias. One year our Christmas event coincided with the worst snowfall we have had while we have lived here. All our opening days throughout Christmas were affected. Deep, deep snow. John dug a path all around the gardens so the treasure hunt for the children could still go ahead. It looked like a winter wonderland. Who needs Lapland? Despite the weather only one family did not make it to the festivities which were truly magical.

John and Malcolm worked well together. They laid the new stone path which runs down to the gate. With some hired help they put the large pergolas into the meadow and planted the roses which now scramble over the structures. It was a sorry day when Malcolm retired but he often pops in to see us. His wife, Margaret, brings her walking club along to The Garden Gate, continuing the support she gave us when she used to come along and volunteer in the gardens.

Roger, our Australian gardener was a very interesting character. He began as a volunteer and shortly afterwards we had a *Gardeners' Question Time* visit. John and I were put in the shade by Bob Flowerdew's knowledge of plant names. Fortunately for us Roger was a good match for him. He joined the permanent team soon afterwards. Not only was Roger a knowledgeable gardener but he also had an interest in carpentry so he was a great help in repairing many of the structures which were showing their age, having been built years earlier by my dad or past gardeners.

Roger was instrumental in solving the long standing problem of the leaking pond. It had gone on for years. In dry weather the water level would drop alarmingly, exposing the ugly black liner. Both John and Malcolm had put it down to evaporation which was a credible explanation as the surface area was very large. However, Roger had other ideas. His background included a good deal of knowledge about trees and he had noticed the hawthorn above the pond was dying. With two volunteers he excavated the area above the waterfall and discovered our pump had been pumping water into the field for years. There was an area of luxuriant growth in the field and the hawthorn had died because its roots were continually wet. Problem solved. The pond level has stayed fairly constant ever since. Roger also reshaped the water features in the two ponds and created the fernery out of a gravelled drive at the bottom of the walled garden. We now use that area as an entrance for our weddings and events. John has widened the path in the walled garden so that couples can stroll up or down together. The path looks as if it has been there for hundreds of years, the original part probably has.

While John and Roger were here we purchased a huge stone bench. What a day that was. We bought it from a reclamation yard and loved it, although we felt we had paid over the odds. Little did we know it would cost more to transport it and put it in place than the initial purchase price. The bench is stone, curved with a carved back and sides. It is over ten feet in length and stands over five feet high. We needed to hire specialist moving gear just to get the pieces from the top of the lane to the middle of the garden. Brute force was then required. Six men were needed to move each part of the seat into place.

It took well over six hours for us to do the job and we had lined it up brilliantly. Maggie arrived to survey our work. She stood there and, with her eye for detail, suggested it just needed moving a few inches to the left.

Her suggestion was met with a dismayed chorus of "No way".

So if you sit on that seat enjoying the view just think how much better it would be if moved just a smidgen. Maggie always does.

While I am on the subject of benches we had a couple visiting from the States. They were celebrating their twenty-fifth wedding anniversary. They would be the first to say that they were rather large people. Anyway, they came to see me and told me they were sorry but they had broken a bench. He said they both thought the earth had moved as they gave each other a celebratory embrace. The whole bench gave way and they ended up sprawled on the grass amidst splinters of wooden legs and slats. The reputation of litigious Americans was not in evidence as they were both howling with laughter. Such a lovely couple who left in a good mood and in better shape than the firewood they left behind. They offered to replace it but I told them not to worry.

We were disappointed when Roger left but his ambitions took him to the Lake District to be a head gardener. We were pleased for him so it was a bitter sweet farewell. Again, it's great that he has been back to see us and we have bumped into him on one of our visits to the North West.

★ ★ ★

Our head gardener, Anne, who joined us more recently is the first gardener here who has previously worked in a tourist attraction and her experience is paying dividends. She and John have become a formidable team and are supported by our largest group of volunteers to date. Together they are transforming the gardens, building on the beauty that already existed and adding to the planting. The major objective being to display the gardens to their best, with colour throughout the year. We are delighted with the results of their hard work. After twenty-one years I think we are finally on top of the gardening work. Well at least for now.

★ ★ ★

One morning we had an impromptu team-build exercise; a large branch of a tree had fallen into the pond. Six of us went to pull it out. You could see who, out of the team, led Nicola, who led from the back; me, who preferred to observe and shout words of encouragement; Maggie; and who the team workers were – everyone else. That huge branch was out of the pond very quickly. What a team.

* * *

Jayne, one of our children's entertainers, always used to go that extra mile by creating her own costumes and bringing in all kinds of props, including her pet rabbit, in order to make her contribution that bit more special.

One enduring memory which involves Jayne is of a near-death experience. She was helping me clear the attic of all kinds of clutter. Such random things. There were just the two of us in the room. I was standing with a tray of ebony elephants as she reached for an assegai spear which then fell from the beam it was perched on. I leapt to the side and only just managed to avoid it going right through me. We were shaken but we were able to laugh about it. We imagined the court case and Jayne's defence.

* * *

The team have always been willing to take on a whole variety of chores including helping in the Gardens and painting in the house as well as decorating the rooms for all our events. Everyone has been willing to do whatever has been required to keep the show going and our guests happy.

The sleeping giant, a sculpture in one of the gardens, is another example of our team work. I explained the overall design of the giant, which would be a huge reclining female figure, to the team. Rio, our volunteer, shaped out the soil. Mark, Jayne and others working at the time helped put down the rubble, bricks and stones collected from around the garden. John, our gardener, helped to shape these and put mesh over the entire figure. John and I shaped the cement to create the figure. As the job progressed this reclining female seemed to look less feminine and increasingly masculine – certainly hermaphrodite. It did not matter. The figure was created and, with some cosmetic surgery over the years, has gone from strength to strength. Today, surrounded by aromatic planting, the giant is to be found fast asleep in the area of the gardens called the Quiet Corner.

★ ★ ★

It is worth mentioning some of the other permanent members of our team. Elvis has left the building and he is in the vegetable patch. Elvis is our scarecrow. I used to make a new head from papier mâché every year. When I was more pressed for time I introduced Elvis, a more permanent character made from wood. He seems to be totally at home in between the vegetables. He has his guitar and we gave him a bike just in case he wants to escape or cycle around the gardens when we are closed.

We have also accumulated a menagerie of creatures including stone lions, elephants, and birds and of course our wooden frog.

Talking of animals. I hate cats. I could only just cope with having a dog. I love people not animals. Maggie would never suggest we had a cat but we have acquired one, a stone one. It has sat outside the kitchen door for over fifteen years. It is a delight, no care required and no bother. I do not just hate cats, I think it may be a phobia. So I was not best pleased when new neighbours arrived with not one cat but two. Double trouble.

One of the cats got stuck up a tree. Both Chris, the owner of the cats, and I are scared of heights. Another phobia. So Chris enlisted our Australian gardener to rescue the cat. With great experience of rescuing koala bears from tall trees Roger had all the attributes for the job. Thus, despite it sticking in my throat, the cat was rescued.

I now found myself on first name terms with a cat, an experience I had never had before. This cat, Tamarind, began to spend enormous amounts of time on our property, relaxing on chairs, snoozing in front of the open fires. sidling up to visitors, walking along walls and generally prancing around just to show off. I found it all rather alarming. However, the visitors love Tamarind. The cat seems to have taken up residence. What's more she has appeared in photographs posted on Facebook, in TripAdvisor comments and even in wedding shots. A real crowd pleaser.

I opened the gate for the start of one season and the first visitor was Tamarind. We really needed to put a season ticket around her neck. My feelings towards this cat were obviously changing, as in the past I have considered putting other things around its neck.

Tightly. I found myself listening to a visitor talking admiringly about Tamarind. I think I managed to hide my distaste as I listened to the disturbing monologue about Tamarind's charm. The woman then thanked me, not only for sharing our home with visitors, but also for sharing our cat. My immediate reaction was to wonder if I could sell the cat to the woman. She would disappear from my life and no one need know, but I found myself saying what a lovely addition she has been to the family. Books are often a place for revelations. I have grown to love Tamarind and all the benefits she freely brings to us. No downside. I do not feed her, and certainly do not touch her but she brings such pleasure to so many of our visitors, she is our perennial volunteer.

I seldom see the neighbour's second cat so there's a blessing.

★ ★ ★

As with any business owners we have made mistakes in recruitment but we have also been very successful in this area. I think it was Tony Jacklin, the golfer who said good management is about picking the right people. How true this is and our current staff group bear this out. What a great team they are.

Nicola started as a café manager and is now our director. She has been hugely instrumental in developing the business. She has helped to secure the employment of all of us with her passion for Crook Hall and ensuring that we have visitors throughout the year. She helped us to develop the Hall and Gardens as a hospitality destination as well as a tourist attraction. She has enhanced our food offering, especially the afternoon teas for which we have gained quite a reputation. One woman told Maggie that she had taken afternoon tea all over the world, including the Ritz, and that this one was the best she had ever had.

Kelly, our general manager, has helped to recruit and train some first class team members. She has put in systems and routines to ensure that our high standards are maintained.

Anna has helped to raise the profile of our art exhibitions while Beth has managed both our apartment and café wonderfully well. She works so hard and encourages her team to follow her example.

We will always be indebted to these talented young women. They run the Hall much more professionally than we ever could. With Anne as head gardener and Siobhan as administration manager we have finally found time for ourselves. We are delighted with all the team and have great faith in their abilities to manage the business in our absence. I am sure they often wish our absences were longer because when we are here we cannot help but interfere – although we call it managing.

We see the whole spirit of Crook Hall continuing long after we are gone. Our ethos is based upon the fact that the most important visitors are the ones who left yesterday and those visiting today. We will only continue to succeed by providing ever improving customer service in a well looked after and maintained environment that is both beautiful and memorable. As a Trust it will be protected from becoming just another country house hotel and will continue to provide an oasis for people to find peace and tranquillity in an increasingly more vibrant Durham City. We know, should anything happen to us, the place is in safe hands. Crook Hall and Gardens have changed since we took it over and we think for the better. Once we have gone, its future will be left to others but we think we have done our little bit.

Afterthoughts

When we bought Crook Hall we thought having our home and work on the same site would make life simpler. When we opened the doors to the public we thought looking after the gardens would become easier.

What an illusion. Our life at Crook Hall has been far from easy and at times the work has been all consuming and exhausting.

What have we learnt from our experience? That's a difficult question but I will have a stab at it:

When you fear the worst you are sometimes right.

Don't invite a bird of prey or an owl to your wedding.

Running water is best when you can turn it off – easily.

Your gut feeling is sometimes right.

Contractors who charge to unblock your drains earn every penny.

Rabbits can swim.

Never climb on a mobility scooter without some basic instruction.

Customers can sometimes be wrong but it is best if you let them believe they are right.

There is no gain without some pain and a good deal of sweat.

Don't throw scones at glasshouses, eat them with lots of jam and cream.

A working central heating system should be top of my Christmas list every year.

A roof over your head is one thing but make sure it is weather proof.

Even if you do not believe in ghosts they can still be very scary.

With the benefit of hindsight would we do it again?

Yes, without a doubt. There has been some blood, a lot of sweat and several tears but it has all been worthwhile.

Owners of Crook Hall and Key Events at that Time

1217	*The Manor of Sydgate (Crook Hall) was granted to Aimeric, the nephew of the Archdeacon Aimeric.*
1199	King John was crowned and the Fourth Crusade began
1215	The Magna Carta was signed
1217–1286	*Marmaduke acquired the estate*
1265	Defensive walls were built around Newcastle
1286–1346	*Peter del Croke took ownership and the estate was recorded as Croke Hall. On Peter's death it was inherited by his wife Alice and son Richard and then passed on to Richard's daughters Isabel, Alice, Agnes and Joan and was divided into two.*
1298	William Braveheart Wallace was defeated at Battle of Falkirk
1314	Robert Bruce defeated the English at Bannockburn
1337	The Hundred Years War begins